Parent to Parent:

Raising Kids in Washington

Publication of
The Parents Council of Washington's
Parent to Parent: Raising Kids in Washington
was made possible by a grant from the
James Lessing Kleeblatt Memorial Foundation.

Parent to Parent:
Raising Kids in Washington

Library of Congress catalog card number 97-80760

ISBN 0-9661107-0-6

Printed in the United States of America
by McNaughton Gunn, Saline, Michigan

Book design and production
Lynn Springer, DL Graphics Studio

Cover photo / Michael Tony, TOPIX
Cover design / Lynn Springer, DL Graphics Studio

The Parents Council of Washington
7303 River Road
Bethesda, Maryland 20817

- - - - - - - - - - - - - -
Acknowledgements

We are pleased to present *Parent to Parent: Raising Kids in Washington*, the latest edition of The Parents Council of Washington's Parent Guidebook. This represents the 7th edition of this guidebook, previously titled *Changing Trends*.

The Parents Council is an organization of 57 private and independent schools in the greater Washington, D.C., metropolitan area. It was created in 1964 to foster communication and cooperation among students, parents and the school community. In today's society, with the constant demands and stresses placed on families, this need has become all the more important.

The guidelines and advice contained in *Parent to Parent* apply to all parents, not just those whose children attend our member schools. We hope it will become an invaluable tool to our readers as they confront the challenges and rewards of parenting. Raising children today is an ever changing process and because of that, we intend to update the materials in this guidebook to keep parents abreast of the latest practices, trends and advice to not only survive but also to strengthen the parent-child relationship. We welcome feedback from our readers on any of the topics in this book; sharing our experiences and learning with one another is important to our effectiveness and success as parents.

As in any project of this scope, one person seems to take on the initial job of spearheading the effort. Anne Marie Mack, Chair of the Publications Committee of The Parents Council, was instrumental in identifying the philosophy and topics to be included in *Parent to Parent*. We also would like to extend our appreciation to the many writers and experts who contributed to this book including Bonnie Benwick, Susan Breznay, Julie Cooke, Carol Day, Pat Douglass, Gerri Fehst, Elly Frieder, Patty Gartenhaus, Natalie Hall, Kathy Hamilton, Pat Hardin, Leslie Harps, Donna Hart, Elizabeth Hayes, Judy Heffner, Grigsby Hubbard, Felicia Lightfoot, Ann Martin, Linda McCormick, Karen Moberly, Carol Newman, Jeanne Reid, Ed Sears, and Lena Zezulin.

Many others contributed to this endeavor to ensure a quality product including B.J. Bralower, Anne Collins, Bob Condit, Michelle Fill-Seele, David Frieder, Robin Goldstein, Lori Goodman, Barbara Harvey, Patty Howie, Linda Jessup, Marguerite Kelly, Laurene McKillop, Dr. Carlotta G. Miles, Patty Myatt, Dr. Betty Ann Robertson-Tchabo, Deborah Rothman, Patricia Elam Ruff and Bobbi Salthouse.

We were extremely fortunate to have received a grant for the initial production of this publication from the James Lessing Kleeblatt Memorial Foundation. Betsy Kleeblatt, a former Board member of The Parents Council, was instrumental in previous editions of *Changing Trends*. We greatly appreciate the Kleeblatt Foundation's invaluable support for our current publication, *Parent to Parent*.

Last, but certainly not least, the finished product would not have been possible without the fine editing of Sandy Burt, the creative design of Lynn Springer and the constant excellence supplied by Dr. Donna Hart, the Executive Editor of *Parent to Parent*. Donna's many years of experience as an editor, writer and educator have been invaluable to all of us who have labored, under her guidance, to produce this book. Donna's leadership made this an educational and tremendously enjoyable experience. Her enthusiasm, creativity and sensitivity were models for us all and no words can express our deep gratitude for her innumerable hours of toil on *Parent to Parent*. This book represents a labor of love by all who were involved, but none more so than Donna Hart.

Elly Coupe Frieder & Elizabeth Haile Hayes
CO-PRESIDENTS OF THE PARENTS COUNCIL

- - - - - - - - - - - - - -

Contents

Introduction

Parent to Parent: Raising Kids in Washington is a publication of The Parents Council of Washington. Its precursor, *Changing Trends,* was first released in the mid-1960s (with five subsequent updates, the last in 1988) as one way to provide you relevant and usable information and resources about issues of common concern to area parents.

Parent to Parent provides current, solution-oriented information and resources to allow us a sense of confidence, satisfaction and pleasure in our role as parents. It identifies concerns, not just "within the family," but important social issues which affect everyone in the independent and other school communities. This guidebook is designed to serve as a common point of reference within our community, a practical guide to active parenting. Informed, thoughtful parents will be prepared for those difficult times when their child presents (or is presented with) a real challenge.

This new edition reflects the reality of the Washington area as an intense, success-oriented, fast-paced place in which to raise a family. Our children are frequently reared in isolated, nuclear families, and they, as well as we, rely more and more on our school communities to be our "neighborhood."

We encourage you to discuss the issues presented in this book with other parents and with your children. Tell your kids, "This book suggests that 'parents should know how the coaches stand on weight loss for sports'." Get your child's point of view; make decisions together. We will be successful if *Parent to Parent* encourages further communication between and among families.

Parenting is an active process. Children develop and mature and as parents we continue to "grow into" our roles. We may find certain stages of childhood (infancy, toddlerhood, adolescence) particularly challenging. Connecting with other parents, individually or in parent peer groups, is essential in order to learn what is "normal" for each period our children go through. This guidebook is another source of information and support .

Parent to Parent is based on the premise that we parents are seeking solutions to the everyday issues involving our children. The "answers" are seldom found in a list of easy steps, but rather are the result of really knowing our children, recognizing the unique learning styles, personalities, temperaments and the levels of maturation that define both our children and us!

Major themes

You may read this book cover to cover in one sitting, pick it up from time to time to peruse or seek its guidance when an issue arises in your family or your community. Regardless of which chapters you read, you will note certain themes which we believe are among the most basic elements of healthy, happy family life. On occasion, and under the everyday stress of life, we can lose sight of these elements. We offer you these overall guidelines, which are addressed in more depth throughout *Parent to Parent*:

- We shouldn't assume that the preteen and teen years will be a trying time for our families. While most kids have some difficult-to-live-with months, this time can be exhilarating–we are watching young adults being formed.

- There are no "right" answers, only possibilities to choose from. Effective parenting involves being aware of our choices. However, remember that some behaviors of our children, as well as the way we handle those behaviors, affect the greater community.

- On a daily basis, we are building people. To paraphrase Marguerite Kelly, noted syndicated columnist and author, schools may give our children their degrees, but we parents give them their character, and that is the gift that matters most.

- We must remember that our children are individuals–respect, accept, support, love and recognize them for who they are.

- We need to be aware of what is "normal"; knowing about expected developmental stages lets us recognize when our child's behavior or attitudes signal "trouble." Another vital part of loving our children is knowing when to go outside the family for help.

- Children growing up in a family with a positive outlook are children with a big advantage in life. If *we* have it, it's infectious.

- When we apologize for our mistakes, we give our children permission to err and to learn from their experiences.

- Our growth is helpful to our children. As they watch us handling our own difficult choices, our children are learning how to handle theirs.

- Remembering we are models, our words and behavior need to reflect our values of equity and fairness. We must teach our children to see the value and worth of every human being, to honor and respect the uniqueness of each person. Respectful, accepting children have learned their values at home.

- Stand up against any kind of stereotyping by gender, race, ethnicity, age, disability, sexual orientation, etc. We shouldn't allow sarcastic, belittling or humiliating comments to get past us without commenting on their negative, often painful impact.

- "Bringing up our children to be good," advises psychologist Erik Erikson, means you "have to keep doing that, bring them up, and that means bringing things up with them: asking; telling; sounding them out; sounding off yourself...." Many well-intentioned parents think there is a time when certain kinds of conversation should, or will, take place. However, our children are being exposed to all sorts of information at a very early age. If we don't jump in, they'll learn "X" from another source. The good news is that most kids want their parents to help distill information and to bring values and openness to a discussion.

- Communication with our children is important. Sometimes it can be on the phone, sitting side-by-side in the car, by e-mail or in the dark just before sleep. We need to talk with our children, early and often, and to practice listening, *really* listening. "The family meal is the foundation of civilization," Miss Manners of *The Washington Post* recently proclaimed. The opportunity is presented nightly.

- Regardless of what they may say, our kids still worry about what we think during their preteen and teen years. It is especially important during these years when peer relationships can be so unstable that our children feel secure with their family.

- Love *is* everything. Every time we kiss or hug our children, we give them the love they need to feel strong and important. Unconditional love from parents is the basis of the "self-esteem" we hear so much about. Our children should feel they can depend on us—even if they have done something we don't approve of. We can love our child and hate the behavior.

- Love includes tough love. We can't permit our children to do things that are not in their best interest. It is important to be able to say *no* and mean it. During adolescence the stakes can be very high. Children, even 17-year-olds, want and need limits.

- We need to remember that parenting is not a popularity contest. Our children may not agree with our viewpoint or be happy when we enforce the consequences of their actions. But we will have given them something much more valuable—an active, caring parent.

- Like plants, children take time to grow. Sometimes we forget that our children need time to dream and aspire—as much as they need activities to keep them busy. We needn't watch the clock, but rather enjoy the scenery.

- Like careers, family life requires lots of time to develop. Parenting skills do too. The idea that quality time is as good as quantity time is misleading. We need to spend as much time with our children as we can, every day.

- If faith is a source of strength to us, we need to share it with our children. The National Longitudinal Study on Adolescent Health reports that if teens understand their parents' belief system and incorporate "that religiosity, spirituality and religious identity it can be protective against early sexual activity and substance abuse." It can also give our children a sense of meaning and purpose.

- All children are "ours." Only when children feel that other grown-ups care, do they feel valued in their own community. This is a job we all do together.

Resources

Because information is a first step in understanding an issue, we have included selected resources such as books, brochures, centers, and workshops at the end of some chapters, as well as a broader listing of recommended resources at the end of the book. We have not listed individual counselors, tutors, therapists, and other professionals. Remember, when seeking information or professional help, a trusted friend, family doctor or school staff member are reliable sources for referrals.

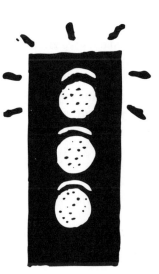

Alcohol & Other Drugs

The junior high school parents attending the high school open house were clearly dismayed by one mother's story of the prevalence of drug and alcohol use in an area high school.

"I'll admit it. When my oldest daughter was a sophomore in high school, I snooped! I listened in on a conversation between my daughter and her best friend. And was I ever glad I did! My daughter's friend was planning to have a party while her parents were out of town. She planned to invite about 30 kids, but knew a few more kids probably would show up. Someone's older brother was planning to supply a keg of beer; somebody else probably would bring some marijuana. It was going to be the best party ever!…

"**. . .** **W**hen I told the girls the party was not going to happen, they were angry. I was being mean and unfair. I would ruin their social lives forever! But I sat them down and explained how quickly things can get out of control, how 30 kids can turn into a hundred, how her parents would be liable if somebody got hurt, how her house could be destroyed by a bunch of kids who got drunk and threw up all over the place, how they would have to clean up all the vomit the next day. They honestly thought that if they just asked the other kids to stay out of the living room and not spill anything on the carpet that her parents would never know! They honestly believed that nobody would get too drunk!

"And my daughter was a "good kid." She was an honors student. She got into a great college. She's planning to go to med school. But this incident is still proof that very bright kids can do very stupid things. Because they are young. Because they want to try new things. Because 'everybody else is doing it'."

Almost all kids will try an alcoholic drink while they are in high school. Lots of them will try drugs. Don't fool yourself into thinking that your kid is somehow going to be immune.

Know the facts

The Family Support Center, an independent, non-profit organization in Bethesda established to support school communities in the Washington metropolitan area, reports the following:

- Of all high school seniors nationwide 80.9 percent reported having experience with alcohol. Nearly half have had a drink in the past 30 days. Three in ten admit having five or more drinks in a row at least once in the past two weeks.

- Nearly one in three teenagers has ridden with a drunk driver. One in four admits driving after using drugs or drinking.

- Drinking and driving are a leading cause of teen deaths. Car crashes account for 40 percent of the deaths of 15- to 19-year-olds. Half of those deaths are alcohol-related. On an average weekend night, one in every ten drivers is legally drunk.

- Nearly one out of five seniors is a daily cigarette smoker. One out of ten smokes a half-pack or more a day by graduation.

- More than 30 percent of seniors admit having tried an illicit drug at least once before they graduate.

- Fifty-seven percent of students say it would be very easy for them to get marijuana. One in four says getting cocaine would be easy.

- In 1993, 17 percent of seniors reported they had used inhalants (glues, gases and sprays).

- Forty percent of adolescents who attempt suicide are drug and/or alcohol users.

Family values

Every family must confront the issues of alcohol and drugs and decide how to deal with them. Different families will make different decisions. Some will decide that the occasional glass of wine at a family celebration is okay. Others will take the stand that they would rather have their teenagers drinking at home than in some unknown location and then driving home. Still others will take a zero-tolerance stand and enforce their policy with their own random drug testing. Be prepared for the fact that your family's values may conflict radically with those of your children's friends, even parents you have known and respected for many years.

Experts say a key component in setting standards for your family is communicating with your child. Adolescents often tell counselors that parents have not taken a stand and often wish that parents had said, "no," clearly and firmly. Counselors also say that failing to follow through on a promised consequence is often more damaging than having no consequences at all.

Some common sense guidelines are set out in the Family Support Center's *Parent Guide Book*. They include:

- Getting to know our child's friends and their parents.

- Knowing where our child is and letting her know where you are.

- Taking a firm anti-drug and anti-alcohol stand.

- Setting and enforcing curfews for weekdays and weekends.

- Being awake when our child comes home after an evening out or asking him to awaken us when he arrives.

- Assuring our child that she can telephone for a ride home whenever needed.

- Calling to verify activities our child plans to attend; being sure our child has actually been invited to the parties in question; finding out if they will be parent-supervised; asking the parents for an assurance that they will serve no alcohol and that they will not permit guests to bring alcohol.

- Calling the parents of boys and girls we suspect to be high, stoned or drunk; being willing to provide a ride to protect them; calling the police if necessary.

- If we will be away overnight with our child at home, having a clear understanding with him that our home is off-limits for parties; alerting neighbors that we will be away and telling them how to reach us if they notice activity that concerns them.

- Telling our children we have asked the neighbors to be available for them while we are gone.

The Family Support Center also suggests the following guidelines for party-giving:

- *Set ground rules.* Our child needs to know what we expect and why we are setting ground rules.

- *Let your presence be known.* If hosting a party, be visible. Do not allow party crashers into our home; things can quickly get out of control.

- *Know your responsibilities as parents.* It is illegal to offer alcohol to guests under the age of 21 or to allow guests to use drugs in our home. Criminal charges may be brought or monetary damages assessed in a civil lawsuit for furnishing alcohol or other drugs to a minor.

- *Limit party attendance and times.* Small groups are easier to handle. Open-hour parties are difficult to control. Other parents will appreciate limits that ensure teens are home at a reasonable hour.

- *Do not allow guests to come and go.* This will discourage teens from leaving the party to drink or use other drugs elsewhere and then returning.

- *Be alert to signs of alcohol and drug use.* If we serve punch, taste it occasionally.

- *Be prepared to ask the guests to leave* if they try to bring drugs or alcohol or if they fail to observe other rules.

- *Notify the parents of any guest who arrives drunk or stoned.*

- *Never let anyone drive under the influence* of alcohol or other drugs, even if it means taking the car keys and calling a cab or asking a sober adult to give the teenager a ride home.

And what if all our good planning goes awry and our child comes home drunk or stoned? That night we should:

- Try to remain cool and calm.

- Find out what she has taken and under what circumstances.

- Call a doctor or take our child to a hospital if she is incoherent or quite ill.

- Tell her we will talk about it in the morning.

- Send her to bed and check frequently during the night.

We should NOT:

- Shout at, accuse or physically abuse our child. This is quite useless in his condition.

The next day we need to:

- Have him assume responsibility for his actions, including clean-up.
- Try to find out the circumstances under which he came to use the drugs and alcohol and who else was there.
- Follow through with the consequences–if they had been previously established.
- Let him know that we do not condone that behavior and will be watching more closely from now on.
- Set new guidelines for our child's behavior, including curfews, insisting upon compliance.
- Consider alternative activities to avoid repeating exposure to drugs or alcohol.

We should NOT:

- Have a discussion with our child if we are too angry to talk about it without losing our temper. Wait until we can discuss it calmly.
- Try to hide the incident from other members of the family.

If you feel overwhelmed, seek help. Many resources are available in the Washington metropolitan area that can help children and their parents deal with substance abuse.

How to know when it's a serious problem

Jacquelyn Horton of the Open Door Runaway Program in Rockville says the first giveaway is a change in behavior. "When they start to change their style and you start hearing the names of new kids you don't know and that you never have a chance to meet, you need to be very concerned," she said.

Other telltale signs include less caring and involvement at home, lack of motivation, frequent irritability, periods of paranoia, and unexplained mood swings. These may be associated with school attendance problems, sharp decreases in grades and an increased need for money. Experts say to be on the lookout for red eyes, unexplained skin rashes, increased acne, persistent coughs, frequent colds and changes in sleep or eating habits.

It is during the middle school years that many children, especially boys, begin experimenting with drugs and alcohol. One study reports that 13 percent of eighth-graders have tried marijuana. For some, it's simply that–an experiment. For a few, it is the beginning of a life-long pattern of social and recreational chemical use. But for others, the consequences are far more dire. Experimentation becomes regular use. Regular use may grow into a daily preoccupation and a state of dependency, where being high is the norm.

Horton says that breaking that dependency requires tremendous work on the part of the entire family. "Parents come into counseling and ask, 'What do I have to do to get my little boy or my little girl back?' They have to work very hard. Recovery takes commitment from the entire family. Often with kids who have gone through two or three rehab programs and where nothing seems to work, we find out that the parents themselves are enabling the addiction." Parents have to make sure their kids get help and that they get help for themselves as well.

Most of all, parents need to realize that kids are using drugs and alcohol to sedate themselves and to escape. "It stems from pain and parents need to find out how to get to the root of it," Horton said. As parents, we need to prepare our children to function successfully in the world rather than to escape from it.

RESOURCES

ALANON & ALATEEN: DC & MD (202) 882-1334; VA (703) 764-0476

Alcoholics Anonymous: DC & MD (202) 966-9115; VA (703) 281-7501

Cocaine Hotline: 1-800-COCAINE

Family Support Center: (301) 718-2467

Narcotics Anonymous 24 hour Hotline: 1-800-234-0420; DC (202) 399-5316

National Clearinghouse for Alcohol and Drug Information: (301) 468-2600

Parents Association to Neutralize Drug & Alcohol Abuse (PANDAA): (703) 750-9285

Toughlove: VA (703) 255-0575; MD (301) 972-2847, (301) 530-3597

See also: Beach Week, Depression, Eating, No!, Parties, Risky Business, Sexual Responsibility, Stress

Alone & Latchkey

"The presence of parents at home at 'key times'—in the morning, after school, at dinner and at bedtime—made teenagers less likely to use alcohol, tobacco and marijuana."

National Longitudinal Study of Adolescent Health

O ur children are growing up in a world of increased juvenile crime, teen pregnancy, sexual assault and depression. Dr. Thomas Long, Catholic University psychologist and long-time researcher of "latchkey" kids, observes that these occurrences parallel an increase in the number of children in self-care and a decrease in caring adult attention.

In the metropolitan Washington area, three-quarters of households with children have either a working single parent or two parents with jobs. Many children take care of themselves before or after school, in the evenings, on weekends or during vacations. Parents either convince themselves that their child will be all right or they go off to work each day feeling guilty and worried.

Some parents become less worried about their children when their children get to be 11 or 12 years old, assuming that their children have what it takes to be alone. Other parents, perceiving more danger, consider quitting their jobs or arranging part-time employment so they can be home with their young adolescent, even though the child protests that the parent's presence is more interference than assistance.

Connectedness

Feeling "connected" to their parents–feeling loved, understood and important–is the most important way to inoculate teens against problems such as drugs and alcohol, attempting suicide, engaging in violence or becoming sexually active at an early age. Even if we work, our children need to have a parent keeping in touch with them, as well as their being able to reach us quickly in an emergency or just to deal with momentary loneliness. In addition, children need parents who come home and show true interest in their day–sometimes a tall order if our own days are long and stressful.

Research has documented that the psychological connection–family closeness–is more important than the physical one. The impact of the "latchkey" experience on kids of all ages depends to a large degree on the strength of the parent-child relationship, and how deeply the kids feel their parents' presence and concern even though the adults are absent. While the number of people working at home is increasing, this does not guarantee that more of us will be home "connecting" with our children. From his 20 years of researching self-care kids, ages 12-16, Dr. Long suggests we need a change of attitude to accompany that trend–being "at home" should mean interacting with the kids, truly "being there for them." Those of us who are able to work at home must build-in time to be involved with, listen to, talk with our children, who are probably in other parts of the house, or our kids will still be in self-care!

Studies have been inconclusive as to whether there is a real difference between self-care and adult-care children on such measures as self-esteem, a feeling of control over events, and behavior. "There is a difference," states Dr. Long, "we just haven't investigated enough. Children who are less supervised are more alone and therefore more likely to get into trouble." Researchers agree that 10- to 15-year-olds are the ones most likely to be negatively affected by the latchkey experience. In some ways they are more vulnerable than younger kids.

What are the issues?

After school programs. Many after school programs, recreation centers and sports organizations provide extracurricular activities for young adolescents which can extend the length of time that children are in what parents may consider "care." However, almost none of the staff of such programs consider themselves to be sitters–they seldom report a child's absence nor do they wait around until every child is picked up.

Transportation. Even if an appropriate program exists, getting there can pose a serious barrier to many children. Public transportation may be non-existent or too time consuming to be considered. And with fewer supervised extracurricular activities now that some schools have downgraded their athletic programs, young adolescents have a whole lot of opportunities to get into mischief at movie theaters, restaurants, billiard halls, food courts or while just "hanging out" at the malls.

Structuring time. Children who are home alone often have difficulty structuring their time. As a result, they may watch too much television, overeat, fight with siblings and experience fear or loneliness. Kids also do lots of things they wouldn't be allowed to do if a parent were around–and parents seldom know about them. This is especially true when children are alone for long periods of time. Whether 7 or 17, they are curious and frequently bored. When left alone for any length of time they may search through drawers and closets. Private areas in the house are particularly interesting, and there is usually little trace of these furtive "explorations."

Gender differences. "There are gender differences when it comes to self-care," reports Dr. Long. When parents tell their children, "Stay at home," they assume the kids will do it. Two-thirds of girls in self-care report that they stay home and do things around the house. Boys almost universally report that they go out from time to time. Both boys and girls are known to forget to close the door behind them.

Having a friend of the same sex over can help parents and kids feel safer and more secure. Girls are likely to stay home and study, talk, cook, paint their nails, listen to music, talk on the phone or online. Dr. Long warns that when a boy has a same-sex friend drop in "to study," one thing can lead to another and mischief (or worse) can occur. Boys are more likely to offer another boy access to the household liquor; the visiting boy may feel there is less danger because it's not his home. In addition, often boys go out–almost guaranteed if the friend has a car.

When a friend of the opposite sex drops in, sexual experimentation, including intercourse, may occur.

Rules. Kids know the rules; they just ignore them, asserts Dr. Long. Telling teens, "Don't do it!" is just not enough. We say, "Stay in the house," "Don't watch TV for hours" and "Don't answer the phone." They say "Yeah, yeah, yeah." When parents or other caring adults are not around, children don't necessarily do what they have been instructed. In their burgeoning quest for independence, adolescents are especially likely to ignore or "modify" their parents' rules.

Problems and solutions

While most kids of ten years or so say they "want to be home alone," few children–even teenagers–would choose to stay alone regularly. They would rather have the comfort of an adult nearby. A child left on his own can become bored, lonely, scared, or must contend with household mishaps. He may hear strange noises or worry about frightening events he's seen on the news. Even his parents' warnings can be alarming. "Don't go outside," "Don't answer the door," "Never tell a caller I'm not home."

Kids in self-care have more numerous and significant kinds of problems because they are alone. Children home alone may get harassing phone calls, often from their own schoolmates. Families may find that "Caller ID" is a useful way for their children to monitor unwanted calls and avoid answering the telephone if they don't recognize the phone number.

"As our daughters mature and blossom sexually, people observe them," cautions Dr. Long. Children are frequently news hounds and hear vivid accounts of children being stalked–and worse. Some families find that a security system makes them and their children feel safer.

Fear and loneliness can be the most distressing problems for many preteens and teens. While most eight-year-olds will be frank and say, "It's scary," older kids won't tell us they are afraid. They say "It's boring." We need to reassure our children that it's all right to say "I'm afraid, to be alone too long/after dark/when it storms." We then must *be there* before it's dark, stormy or "too long."

Sibling care

We often see our older children as substitute childcare. Girls are more often given the responsibility of caring for their younger siblings. When boys are charged with care-giving, they are still more likely to be out and about. Adolescent boys may be seen as threatening by their sibs, warns Dr. Long, as the older brother may sometimes experiment with being rough and even sexual with them. When an older sibling of either gender is "in charge" and trouble with the younger kids ensues, the teen will do what he's seen adults do—talk, threaten, yell, or smack.

Children caring for siblings need to be even older and more mature than other children ready for self-care. The younger siblings need to be comfortable about staying home with their older brother or sister. Self-care and sibling-care need to be carefully considered if one child has special needs or if the children are adjusting to new family circumstances such as separation or divorce.

When we expect our children to regularly care for themselves as well as younger siblings, they may feel that we are avoiding our adult responsibilities and become resentful.

Communication

Regardless of their age, children can manage better on their own, for a limited time, if we take the time to prepare them adequately. Being able to talk with each other is a basic prerequisite and is best established long before the child is a teenager. We need to ask ourselves: How much do my child and I talk? How likely is she to tell me what's really going on? Most kids tell their parents what they want to hear. Most parents are not privy to as much as we think, and don't know how little we know.

Being in touch with our children is an essential ingredient to their comfort and confidence, their safety, and their ability to keep out of trouble. We can call our children frequently from work and as soon as we expect them home. The very best way to know where our children are and what they're up to, Dr. Long recommends, is to call them first—don't wait for the kids to call us. Parents should call and say, "I'm thinking of you," "How was your day?" "What did you find for a snack?" "What homework do you have?"

We need to make ourselves more accessible to our children with the use of pagers, cellular phones and voice mail. If they know that we can always be reached, some of the stress of being alone will be relieved. In addition, we can identify a person, preferably in the neighborhood, to call if a problem or emergency arises. Prominently post by the telephone work numbers, fire, police, extended family members, neighbors and friends' numbers. Some parents also post their home address, believing that a child could become too emotional to remember this essential piece of information in a true emergency. Our neighbors should know how to reach us at work.

We shouldn't inadvertently communicate to callers that no adult is home. We might consider the content of our phone message–instead of a phone message that says, "We are not home right now," say "We can't get to the phone," or, "We're on another line." Few children lie well–especially if a caller is persistent in requesting their parents come to the phone. Even teenagers stumble all over themselves when explaining why their (absent) parent cannot take the call.

Preparation

We need not only to instruct, but also to offer "what if" scenarios to prepare young adolescents for unusual circumstances. Planning should include what to do when feeling bored, what homework and house responsibilities to do; how to handle peers who show up unexpectedly; how to interact with friends; how to answer the phone. Even teens may have difficulty dealing with the unexpected. Role play for such occurrences as strangers knocking at the door or the electricity going out.

Model the appropriate way of doing things around the house. We assume that telling our kids the rules and showing them how to do things once or twice will suffice, but even teenagers don't always internalize our instructions.

If we allow our child to go outside or leave home, we should give clear instructions as to when and where he can go. Our teen will likely go out sometimes. Work out with him how to keep us informed about his whereabouts. This is especially true when a teen has a car–or a friend with a car. Calling us before leaving and upon arriving at different destinations is a good rule. Giving a child a cellular phone to carry when out and about, limiting its use to parent communication can be a valued investment. We need not accept, "I was just over at Jamie's." Asking questions shows our child that we care and are concerned despite our absence.

A more commonplace occurrence that transcends ages and causes kids in self-care distress is losing essentials–keys, coats, books. A contingency plan for lost keys, a secret hiding place for spare keys or keys entrusted with a few neighbors who are usually available can remove one cause of stress.

Even if our child does seem ready for self-care, we will need to think about some other factors: Is our home safe? Is our neighborhood safe? How long will our child be alone each day? Is there a place nearby where an adult lives or works where our child can go for help? Does our child have special medical, physical or emotional needs? Is our family going through a difficult transition period due to a recent move, death, divorce or remarriage?

Overnight alone

It is never a good idea to leave a preteen or teen at home alone overnight. If we cannot arrange care for our children, either we shouldn't go or we should take them with us, advises Dr. Long. Kids need to have adult supervision. The big danger is not that our child will invite 50 people to party, but that word will get around that "Jeremy's parents are out of town" and 35 kids will show up with a keg for a spontaneous party.

Teenagers are not able to control what their friends, and particularly a "gang" of other teens, do. They get embarrassed about having to restrain them or unable to stop fighting, noise, or kids pairing into bedrooms. We need to help them learn how to avoid problems with strict guidelines for calling a responsible adult to help at the first sign of a party invasion. Their primary protection is an adult consistently on site.

No matter how well we prepare them, children alone are facing the unknown alone. We must go over "adult stuff" multiple times to ensure that our teens will integrate rules and precautions. Dr. Long reminds us that taking care of ourselves is an adult task; it takes years to be good at it.

See also: Alcohol, Beach Week, Gender, Parties,
Risky Business, Sexual Responsibility

Anger: Learning to Control It

Intense feelings such as anger and frustration can be scary for adolescent and parent alike. "But anger is conquerable if you and your child learn how to handle it," points out Britt Rathbone, director of Rathbone & Associates, a Bethesda outpatient mental health practice for adolescents. "It's a signal that some need is not being met, that some boundary is being violated or crossed," explains Washington therapist Susan Drobis. Anger provides valuable information. And it's certainly part of every teenager's life. Unfortunately, parents often don't know how to help their children manage their anger, and, in fact, may not handle their own anger well.

Understanding anger and its triggers

When we perceive a threat, our bodies react with the "fight or flight" syndrome. We produce a burst of adrenaline, our hearts pump more blood to muscles, and in effect we get ready to fight off an attack or run away. We react the same whether we feel physically or emotionally threatened.

Adolescents' lives are full of physical and emotional threats. Control battles with parents, restrictions on their freedom, competition between siblings, the pressure of school and homework, anxiety about a test or getting into college, the need to separate from parents, an argument with a friend, feeling fat or stupid or unloved, dating problems, social injustice, the inequities of everyday life, feeling mature but not being treated that way... it's a wonder that adolescents and preadolescents aren't angrier than they are!

Helping children understand what triggers their anger is the first step to helping them manage the anger. Each person's triggers are unique. "If somebody comments on an area that we're struggling with or feel vulnerable about, we feel threatened," Rathbone points out. "When we feel threatened, we get angry." We also get angry at what we think is not fair, or when we don't feel respected. Anger within the family is sometimes triggered by the individual or collective fatigue of parent and child.

Understanding what triggers anger is complicated by the fact that the anger may be covering up another emotion. Fear, anxiety, rejection, hurt, or feelings of helplessness may lie beneath the anger. Professional help is sometimes needed to identify what's truly triggering a person's anger.

Managing anger

No matter what triggers the feeling, anger itself is a normal, healthy emotion. Parents can help their children (and themselves) learn to manage anger and channel it into constructive outlets with these steps:

Set boundaries or rules about anger. A family's values will determine what rules about anger are acceptable to that family. Some people can tolerate door slamming or swearing, while others can't. "Anything that feels abusive, whether directed at a sibling, a parent, or someone else, is destructive," Drobis cautions, and should not be tolerated.

Differentiate between feelings and behavior. When setting limits, separate emotions and actions. Anger, an emotion, is normal. Your child needs to know that it's okay to feel angry, to express angry feelings, but it's not okay to hit or hurt people or property. When setting rules about anger, be clear about what behavior is unacceptable in your family.

Listen to let your child blow off steam. When kids are most worked up and upset, you can diffuse a lot of their anger simply by listening empathetically, using validating phrases such as "I can see that you're angry." Don't get agitated or upset while your child is venting, Drobis advises. This can be difficult to do, particularly when you disagree strongly with what your child is saying. "But you can be empathetic and understand that this is the way they see a situation, without having to agree with what's being said."

Encourage your child to talk about his anger. "Stuffing" intense emotions such as anger is not good; the anger will go underground, only to surface at some other time. While many individuals are not comfortable talking about such intense feelings, parents can encourage their kids to do so. Marguerite Kelly, local author of the syndicated column "Family Almanac" and several parenting books including *The Parent's Almanac,* suggests introducing discussions about anger in situations that feel safe to your child. Try talking with your child on the phone, in the dark, when you're working side by side in the kitchen, or in the car–a particularly effective site for privacy.

Don't discount the emotion. "Children have to be able to express their opinions openly," Kelly observes, without having a parent discount or dismiss their anger. A parent who says, "Of course your teacher likes you," is, in effect, saying to the child, "You don't know what you're talking about."

Identify the reason for the anger. "No child has a behavior that doesn't have a reason," points out Kelly. "Get to the bottom of the anger and frustration." Be an active listener; listen beyond the words to get to the child's true meaning. Check out what you think you hear. "I sense that you're angry because I said you had to come home early. Is that correct?"

Beware of reacting to anger. Shouting matches aren't good for anybody. But parents are human, and may find themselves reacting to their child's anger. "If you can catch yourself in time," Drobis suggests, "find a sense of humor and say, "Let's erase the beginning of this scene and start over again.'" Other times, you may need to give yourselves time to regroup. "Know when it's a good time to withdraw," Kelly says. For example, the parent might say to the child, "We're both saying things we're going to be sorry about later. Let's both pull ourselves together and meet here in 15 minutes to talk some more."

Teach kids to reassess an anger-causing situation. "Our emotions are based on our thoughts," therapist Rathbone points out. "How we assess a situation brings about an emotion." He suggests that parents help kids reassess situations that have provoked angry feelings, as in the following scenario:

"You think Alex treats you like a loser. How so?"

"He threw a spitball at me yesterday."

"Has he ever thrown a spitball at anybody else?"

"Well, yeah, he got in trouble for throwing a spitball at Sarah last week."

In this situation, the teen begins to understand that Alex is not singling him out or picking on him alone. Such an approach, Rathbone says, can help a child put an anger-producing situation in perspective and determine whether their angry reaction is appropriate to the situation.

Help your child problem-solve. Help a child find a solution to her problems after she's calmed down. "Anger is like wax in the ears," Kelly explains. "Kids can't hear you if they haven't gotten rid of their anger" first. When they have, suggests Drobis, "be available to help them to problem-solve, rather than loading them up with advice." Coach them to find their own solutions. Use encouraging statements such as "I know you'll work this out" or "You'll make the right choice."

Help your child develop anger outlets. Show kids how to develop safe ways to express their feelings, and to understand that the feelings themselves are not dangerous or bad. Constructive outlets for their anger can include listening to loud music, singing at the top of their lungs, hitting some tennis balls, calling a friend, punching a pillow, writing an angry letter (and then throwing it out), or writing in a journal. What's important is that the angry feelings themselves not be seen as dangerous or bad, but rather are channeled into a safe outlet.

Suggest distractions. Sometimes, when adolescents get angry, they may get stuck on a thought and keep replaying it over and over. "Suggest that they listen to a tape, read a book, do homework, or get together with their friends. Chances are they'll come back without that heightened sense of irritation and anger," recommends Rathbone. However, returning to the same issue may be a necessary part of the process of "working it out"; support whatever process seems to be most productive for your child. If your child is one who needs to stew, coach him or her how to let go of anger.

Talk about anger. Look for teachable moments, suggests Rathbone. Talk about what you and your teen observe on the street, on television or in the movies. Get your child thinking about anger with questions such as "What do you think about what he did? Have you ever done something like that? Is it worth it?" If your child is uncomfortable talking about feelings, draw analogies from something he is interested in. Sports, for example, provide lots of examples of athletes positively delaying their angry impulses and thinking through their reactions.

Use your own anger as an example to discuss anger management techniques –those that work, and those that haven't. Teens know that you get frustrated and angry, too. For example, tell your child how embarrassed you were after you lost your temper when someone pulled into the parking place you were waiting for. Explain that you wished that you had handled the situation differently. Ask your child what he would have done in a similar situation.

Keep an anger log for greater understanding. If your child's anger seems out of proportion in frequency and intensity, it could stem from an underlying cause, particularly emotional distress, or even food allergies. Kelly suggests that recording information for a week or more about your child's anger can provide you and your child with valuable insights into the causes of that anger. In a diary, record your child's behavior, what triggered it, any emotional stress she is under, what the weather is, what the child has eaten, etc. Involve your teen in the process if she is receptive and interested in learning more about what may be causing the anger. If your child's anger persists in frequency or intensity, seek professional help.

Help your child maintain balance. Kids who eat the right food and get plenty of rest and exercise are apt to be more resilient emotionally. "When people exercise regularly, they seem to have a higher threshold for frustration, and don't get angry as easily," Rathbone says. Encourage your child to learn stress management techniques, such as yoga, deep breathing and meditation.

Don't be afraid of your child's anger. "Parents today are afraid of their kids' anger and cave in when the limits they set are challenged," Drobis says. They don't want to face their child's anger or see their kids frustrated. While kids may not be thrilled by the limits that are set, parents need to set appropriate limits to do their job. They have to be strong enough to tolerate their child's frustration and anger. Giving in when your child is angry will not help her develop the anger management tools she needs.

Drobis advises that anger and irritability in a child can be a sign of depression. "Look for other signs, such as sudden changes in behavior or in academic patterns, friendships, or activities." Watch for feelings of low self-esteem. "Any expressions of a child's wishing they were dead needs to be taken seriously," she says. In addition, "if behavior is persistently and consistently destructive and violent, there's something very powerful going on in that child, and the child and the parent may need more help than the parent can provide."

Parents' anger

Manage your own anger. "Most of us were not taught to deal with feelings," Drobis points out. "But parents can't really help a kid learn to deal with anger if they have problems with it themselves." If you find yourself exploding frequently, work at identifying what's triggering your anger. For example, adolescents' attempts to separate and differentiate, and the demands they make for changes in the family, can be particularly troublesome for some parents. It's important that parents understand what's going on developmentally, and to understand that things will settle out eventually. Getting support from friends and partners can help parents survive a difficult time and manage their anger more effectively.

Know when you need help. Parents should seek professional help if their own anger is uncontrollable, or if they find themselves feeling destructive, verbally or physically abusive or violent.

Learn more about anger yourself. Individual and family therapy, parenting and anger management classes and books can help you help your child and yourself manage anger more effectively.

See also: Alone, Depression, No!, Shoplifting, Stress, Vandalism

RESOURCES

Anger management resources for teens and parents: Institute for Mental Health Initiatives, Washington, DC, 202-364-7111.

Anger management videos developed by Mental Health Initiatives include "Anger Management for Parents and Learning to Manage Anger, the RETHINK Workout for Teens". Available from Research Press, Champaign, IL, 217-352-3273.

Anger, The Misunderstood Emotion, Carol Tavris. New York: Simon & Schuster Inc., 1989.

The "Dealing with Feelings" series, including *I'm Furious*, 1992, *I'm Frustrated*, 1992, *I'm Angry.* 1994, Elizabeth Crary, illustrated by Jean Whitney. Seattle, WA: Parenting Press, Inc.

How to Talk so Kids Will Listen and Listen so Kids Will Talk. Adele Faber. New York: Rawson- Wade, 1980.

There's a Volcano in My Tummy: Helping Children to Handle Anger,
A Resource Book for Parents, Caregivers and Teachers, Elaine Whitehouse and Warwick Pudney, Gabriola Island, BC: New Society Publishers, 1996.

Beach Week

Did you hear the one about a group of Washington area teenagers who rented a second floor townhouse in Fenwick Island? Well, actually, one of their mothers rented the house, lying about who would occupy it. During one long evening of celebration–which included a keg or two– the guys lugged the owner's ground level grill up the steps, through the apartment, and onto the balcony. Hours later, police driving by spotted the smoldering balcony. When fire-fighters arrived they had one heck-of-a-time awakening the sleepers–including the one passed out on a lounge chair just a few feet from the flaming deck.

In recent years, beach week has earned a reputation for exposing high school seniors to sex, alcohol and irresponsible behavior. The practice of giving new graduates a chance to relax with the privilege of some independence usually takes place in June; often, this invitation extends to juniors and even freshmen. Whether Washington area teenagers head to Ocean City, Rehoboth, or Virginia Beach, trusting parents feel pressured to let their 16- to 18-year-olds attend. By considering their teen's history and instincts, parents can judge how or whether to sanction a week of independence with peers.

Keys to safe celebrations include adequate numbers of responsible chaperones, much communication among parents, and each

family's thorough preparation of the teenagers who plan to participate. Consider this another "first" for your child and do your part to
make it safe and fun. Parents of graduating seniors sometimes throw
up their hands, saying they really have to *trust* their child who has
"almost left home." This abdication of authority, of actively participating in the plans for a beach trip, could have a high price tag.

What's the danger?

Northern Virginia physicians Cynthia Horner and Richard
Schwartz, who directed a study of how 59 "typical" female high-
school grads spent their beach week in 1996, found that:

- Three out of four reported they "got drunk every day."
- Half reported that they had sex at least once during the week–
  and nearly nine out of 10 said they were drunk at the time.
- One out of six said they or a close friend needed medical attention
  because of injuries suffered while drunk or high.

Beach week can be rife with danger. Teenagers can end up in
situations they cannot control and may receive citations involving
fines for disorderly conduct, public intoxication, violation of beach
laws or noise regulations. They may get pregnant, sexually transmitted diseases, or AIDS. Especially troubling is the inclusion of freshmen, sophomores, and juniors who are less equipped to handle all
that the celebration promises.

Make it safe

Although most schools do not sponsor or sanction beach week
activities, parent groups often offer workshops or meetings about
related safety concerns. If parents are firmly against the practice,
the meeting is a good place to weigh the merits of alternatives such
as chartered bus trips to theme parks or allowing smaller groups of
friends to spend time at family-vacation homes. One local independent school sponsors a beach week for the entire senior class chaperoned by faculty and staff.

Police from the beach areas will come to local jurisdictions in the
late spring with the latest information about how they will handle
safety issues. Due to recent problems with younger aged celebrants,
police in Dewey Beach have actually advised *against* sending teens
to their shores. It is best to check with police in specific jurisdictions
before finalizing plans.

For parents, it is important to be clear and specific with your child about whether you, as a family, think the fun of beach week outweighs its dangers. If you give the green light, be just as clear about how your child is to behave. It's good for parents and teenagers to make beach week living arrangements beforehand, including getting relevant phone numbers and knowing where parents will be.

For teenagers, it is important to choose friends they can trust as beach week cohorts. Those who go must accept the responsibility with full knowledge of the penalties; if a rental house or hotel room is damaged, understand who will pay. All occupants will most likely be held equally responsible even if only a few cause the damage.

For chaperones, it's important to know the children who are going; a meeting beforehand is a good place to agree on guidelines and curfews. It is also a good idea to put those rules in writing for all families involved, and to be clear that drinking is illegal for teenagers in all beach jurisdictions. Experienced chaperones often come equipped with a firsthand knowledge of the territory, maps, suggestions about restaurants, and recreation and shopping.

Getting to the shore involves several hours of driving and parents will want to review who is driving, the routes that will be taken and arrangements for emergencies.

In preparation for a beach trip, review with your teen your family's values and admonitions about sexual activity.

All beach week participants should bring medical insurance information and a signed parental release for emergency medical treatment, so there will be no delay if medical care is required.

Beach week is an extension of the growing opportunities our teens have for making choices. The friends they choose, their ongoing decisions on alcohol and drug consumption, and their self-confidence in a milieu of peer pressure reveal the level of maturity they will bring to beach week. If we have provided the security of clear boundaries and the tools for good judgment throughout our child's growing years, we can feel a little more comfortable consenting to this celebration.

See also: Alcohol, Communicating, Date Rape, Driving, Parties, Risky Business, Sexual Responsibility

Cheating & Honor Codes

Most of the independent schools in our area operate with an honor code that sets forth the basic philosophy of how the members of that school community are expected to act. In addition to having a lower incidence of cheating, such academic settings also foster enhanced acceptance of moral education and community values when there is a well-established and respected code of conduct.

We can all remember back to our days in school when someone was caught cheating. It was a big deal. Many kids today are more jaded when it comes to cheating, and the incidence has increased dramatically. A recent survey of a group of private institutions found that 57 percent of students at schools with honor codes admitted to cheating once or more; at schools where there was no honor code, that number rose to 78 percent.

The child of today who cheats without paying any consequences may carry a similar sense of abandon into his adult professional and personal life. Unfortunately, the consequences of "cheating" as an adult can be severe.

Cheating is stealing

Cheating is the purposeful stealing of another person's work or ideas. It occurs when a student does not do his own work on an academic paper or exam. With today's computer technology, instances of cheating are being expanded to include the following:

- Using research from computer sources without documenting it
- Buying research papers
- Doing homework for someone
- Copying from another's exam
- Allowing a student to copy from your exam
- Preparing notes to take into a closed-book exam (i.e., writing on your hand or desk)
- Using unauthorized resources and claiming them as your own
- Having a parent write (as opposed to minor editing) a paper or do other required homework

Resisting the impulse to cheat

If a student sees others cheating and getting away with it, she may be tempted to try it herself. Research shows that schools with an honor code generally have been successful in creating an environment and attitude which decreases cheating. Equally important is the message that parents send to their children on the subject. Parents need to demonstrate their belief in the "core value" of honesty in their everyday life, such as pointing out the discrepancy when a merchant makes an error in pricing.

When we model honesty in our daily interactions, our children will absorb its importance. You can:

- *Inform your child* about her school's and your own attitudes on cheating and its many forms (i.e. plagiarism, copying homework, exchanging answers).

- *Lighten the pressure* for your child to achieve "good" grades at all cost. Today's kids are constantly reminded of the competitive environment they live in, the push to get into the best high school or college–a possible motivation for cutting corners or taking risks to get better grades.

- *Alert your child* to the possible situations such as a classmate attempting to use his school work or homework in a dishonest manner. Help your child learn how to rebuff such opportunities for cheating.

- *Cooperate with school authorities* to resolve the matter, if your child is caught cheating. Covering up for a child who has cheated prevents learning an important life skill: acceptance of the consequences of one's own actions.

What is honor and how do you "get it"?

Honor involves self-respect and respect for others. It requires us to live in a community that is based on the ideals of honesty, integrity, trust and courtesy. In order for an honor code to "work" (be broadly effective), people in the school community—students, parents, faculty and administrators—must have a sense of responsibility and recognize that there are penalties for violations of the rules.

Honor codes tend to concentrate on the big ticket items at schools—cheating and plagiarism, lying, stealing and damage to property. But in order to succeed, the underlying concept of honor must be emphasized equally at home and school. If we brag about how we "got away with something" on our income taxes or engage in questionable business practices, we are sending a clear message to our child that either there is a double standard of conduct for adults or that honesty in one's personal life is a matter of convenience. A parent who "retypes", i.e., edits or even rewrites his child's required academic papers, is cheating for his child and giving a strong message that it is okay to take credit for work that does not reflect your own ability or understanding.

As children develop, they increasingly accept responsibility for their behavior, at home, school and in the community at large. They can recognize permissible parameters for their actions and accept the responsibility that accompanies greater privilege and freedom. While it is important to recognize that everyone makes mistakes, a mature person is able and inclined to fix them. Though sometimes truthfulness is hard to maintain, honesty is a critical element of the trust necessary for a successful honor code.

As parents, we can encourage our schools to have a rigorously enforced honor code and to make it a key part of student life. At home we shouldn't hesitate to use everyday incidents to teach our child, by example, how honesty and trust are crucial to being an ethical person. Like charity, honesty begins at home.

See also: Anger, Computers, Friendships, Push for Success, Risky Business, Stress

Clubs & Concerts

"**M**om, I'm going to see the "___" (a rock/rap/cult group known only to your teen and his friends) at _____ (guaranteed to be far away or maybe in a "bad" neighborhood). What can we say to this frequent request? Many teens and some preteens love to go to rock concerts and clubs. This can be a good opportunity to hear their favorite artists and also socialize with their peers. So much of their group culture is enhanced or defined by music.

As parents we can take a number of steps to ensure our teens' safety and our own comfort. Some suggestions assume we will join them; others allow us to prepare the kids to attend without us:

- *Be aware of the nature of the concert site or club* and discuss with your children your expectations of behavior and the safety issues that might arise.

- *Know the type of concert and ages of the concert-goers.* In some instances you may be able to go to the concert or club with your child or send him with a reliable group of friends. There are legitimate concerns about teens driving at night with a crowd in the car. Some large facilities, such as USAir Arena, have a waiting area for parents.

- *Be sure one adult and teen know the exact location* of the concert site, the parking facilities, and the time needed to get there and back. Teen drivers need to share this information with other group members and parents. Don't send a group of teens off to negotiate unknown high-ways or city streets at night.

- *Set a curfew*, realizing concerts often start late and traffic can be heavy.

- *Park in a lighted area.* Each person needs to write down where to meet or the car location in case the group gets separated.

- *Consider sending a car phone* along with the group.

- *Leave jackets in the car.* It's hot inside the clubs and they can get lost.

- *Advise your daughter not to take a purse*–use a fanny pack. If your teen wants to take pictures, he can use a camera with a neck strap. (Check the concert's regulations–often cameras and tape recorders are not permitted.)

- *Use ear plugs.* Most big shows are in the 105 to 120 decibel range; ear damage can begin at 85 decibels.

- *Be aware!* Enclosed arenas sometimes are filled with cigarette smoke, posing a problem for teens with allergies or asthma.

- *Hold on to your own ticket under all circumstances.* Some concert facilities have reserved seating inside or under a roof while others have open lawn seating–a much more difficult arrangement for keeping a group together. Some clubs are quite small while arenas, of course, are huge.

- *Bring identification for clubs.* Clubs and concerts attract a broad spectrum of audience, from 12-year-olds through adults. Few clubs discourage underage patrons and even fewer admit only "adults." Hand stamps are used to distinguish underage and legal age. Bar areas check for age. Security is usually tight and those who try to use fake identification or have someone buy drinks for them can be removed. Young women need to be careful because they may be targeted by older guys. In addition, parents need to discuss the legal and parental consequences of drinking and drugs.

- *Avoid the "mosh pit" or area in front of the stage.* People dance, push and shove–a very rough scene. Tell your teens: no stage diving, no crowd surfing, no throwing objects on the stage. Many clubs and arenas have such rules posted.

With precautions, going to a club or concert can be a positive experience. You might even enjoy being a part of their scene for a night!

See also: Alcohol, Communicating, Date Rape, Driving, Risky Business

Communicating & Networking

In bygone days, conversations over the backyard fence provided parents with a rich source of advice, comfort, news, and plain old gossip, on the challenges of parenting. Nowadays, Washington area parents find themselves isolated from such support by carpool rules which keep us in our vehicles, school families living many miles apart, and demanding personal and career schedules which preclude casual conversation with other parents. Many parents have come to realize that their child's school has become their surrogate neighborhood: the school community has replaced the backyard fence.

To state the obvious, communicating with other parents can make a difference. If you are wrestling with a problem or in need of advice about topics ranging from learning disabilities to curfews, from risk-taking behavior to beach week, one thing is certain: other parents are too, and they may well have tried approaches that can help you. But the concept of networking is actually an old-fashioned activity–talking to other parents. It requires more conscious effort than in the era when parents chatted while the kids played ball in the street.

Over the fence

Families' beliefs about parenting and appropriate behavior are different, and they vary further the older children get. How do you deal with the reality that some families permit their 10-year-old to

watch R-rated movies when your child is visiting; that some children are permitted to visit the shopping mall or Georgetown unsupervised and your child wants to go too; that some parents feel comfortable taking a vacation and leaving their 17-year-old home alone and you find out afterwards that your child has attended a party there?
For starters,

Take every opportunity to talk with other parents:

- Volunteer at school, attend parent receptions, back-to-school nights and use such occasions to raise informally parenting topics of concern to you.
- Sit with other parents at school sporting events and performances, and ask their ideas about a current problem.
- Attend parent peer group meetings at school where current developmental issues will be discussed.
- Organize an informal gathering of parents who are dealing with a specific common problem.
- Start communicating with other parents when your child is younger: connections can be harder to make when children are in middle and high school.
- Don't shy away from picking up the phone to discuss a specific concern with another family.

The last suggestion may be the hardest, but there are times when it will be necessary. Remember that different families have different standards; acknowledge the awkwardness of the call, and seek the diplomatic approach. Your child will almost certainly be irritated that you are calling; try to recognize those feelings, try not to embarrass him, but do not be deterred:

Your 16-year-old wants to attend a party at a classmate's and you want to know if the parents will be home...

TRY THIS: You call the family and say, *"It's so nice of you to let Mary host a party this weekend and Kathy is looking forward to coming. I wondered if I could help in any way?"* Needless to say, if Mary's family doesn't plan on being home or even know about the party plans, you will get an answer to your question.

You know that the last time your child spent the evening with the Joneses, they rented what you feel was an inappropriate video for the kids to watch...

TRY THIS: You call the family, and say, *"Thanks so much for inviting John over. How about if we pick up a movie for the kids?"* This could lead to discussion about movies and your limits in a less confrontational way.

Your daughter has a date for dinner, the prom and an after prom party. You feel there is potential for dangerous behavior and bad choices...

TRY THIS: You call the parents of your daughter's date as well as the parents of a number of her friends and say, *"You know we all really want the kids to have a good evening. How about getting together to talk about how we can make sure it's fun and safe."* One real value of such a gathering is that the teenagers will know that their parents have been in communication and are paying attention to their plans.

It is almost always reasonable to doublecheck your child's understanding of what is planned–you can convey your trust and your appreciation for his or her good judgment while doing so. Just as you let your children know your evening's agenda, you can make it clear that you expect the same from them.

Parent peer group format

A more formal strategy for networking is the parent peer group, usually organized and led by parents, but supported and encouraged by the school. One parent, when asked about the value of such gatherings, responded, "Our group has been meeting since our children were in the 5th grade. Now that they are in high school, there is a bond among the parents and we have come to know each other well. We have had parents talk openly about serious problems, and this honesty has been beneficial. Not every meeting has been a wild success, but I have almost always walked away with one new idea. And even if I find parents with whom I disagree, we have had a chance to air our views."

The most successful meetings are those which adhere to certain ground rules. Parents and schools who are seeking to set up or revitalize a parent peer group program might want to read The Parents Council of Washington guidelines and materials, available through the Parents Council office.

Briefly, the following generally accepted procedures have been found to be effective.

- *Parents should wear name tags.*
- *Chairs should be arranged in a circle.*
- *Meetings should begin and end on time.*

- *Do not conduct business at the meeting,* such as recruiting volunteers for school events.
- *Do not permit the meeting to become a gripe session* about school policies.
- *A facilitator should be appointed ahead of time.* (Many schools hold a training session for facilitators–a good idea). This person will be most effective if she has good meeting leadership skills, makes sure that there is wide participation, and enforces the following ground rules:
  - Do not discuss a parent or family who is not there, or individual children. Refer to the general subject, not personalities.
  - Try to make sure that everyone who comes, speaks. Do not let one parent dominate.
  - Move the discussion along so that all topics are discussed.
  - Discussion will focus on social, developmental and family issues about children and parenting.
  - School issues, comments about particular teachers, classes, etc. should be avoided. Such concerns should be discussed with appropriate school personnel.
  - Everything that is said is to be treated with confidentiality.
- *Each meeting begins with parents introducing themselves* around the circle, giving their child's name and suggesting one or two topics that they would like to address during the meeting.
  - Choose one person to act as recorder using a blackboard or newsprint to list the topics for discussion.
  - Commonly addressed topics:

    Early childhood–6th grade:
    Bedtimes, allowance, cliques, discipline, TV and video games

    7th–8th grades:
    Homework, dating, smoking, curfews, movies, limit setting, telephone habits

    9th–12th grades:
    Alcohol and driving, unchaperoned parties, substance abuse, rules for driving, beach week, stress for seniors.
- *Use the topics to proceed with the discussion.* Some topics are similar and can be addressed together. Someone may be asked to serve as timekeeper and announce when 10 or 15 minutes has passed so the next topic can be addressed.

- *Do not take notes.* People will feel they can speak more freely. A simple list of topics discussed at the meeting can be circulated after the meeting.

- *Remember the goal is to communicate,* not necessarily to always provide answers or produce proposals. (Some meetings have, however, produced useful contacts among parents, for instance about parties or prom night.)

- *Have a good time.* Laugh. Make sure that new parents feel welcome.

Communication pays off

There is very little downside to better parent communication, and many benefits:

- If and when a crisis occurs, you will be in a better position to deal with it if you already know the parents of your child's friends. Others will feel more comfortable about confiding in you.

- If you know the parents of your child's friends, and if you talk to them periodically, chances are you will discover that many families are operating under guidelines very similar to your own. This can put an end to such myths as "I'm the only kid in the class who can't stay up 'til midnight." On the other hand, if you learn that some families have standards very different from your own, you will be in a better position to deal with that reality.

- Parents who do network find they are more successful in helping their children avoid risk-taking behavior.

- There is value in kids knowing that their parents are in touch with other parents regularly.

- Finally, remember and be assured, your child does indeed have his own network. Parents need to develop theirs.

See also: Clubs, Driving, Parties, Shopping Malls

Computers: Virtual Family Fun

Traveling in cyberspace, children can find a pen pal, get help with their homework, discover a hobby, become computer savvy and expand their horizons. And that is just the beginning.

Many parents, operating under a technological disadvantage, are struggling to keep up with the "cyberspace smorgasbord" so familiar to their children and often discover that the resources available to them are inadequate. Computer books often are based on the assumption that the reader knows far more than he actually does. And the information provided does not always address parental concerns but rather those of the common user.

Balancing computer use with other activities is a worry to parents, some of whom are concerned that their children may become obsessed with computing. Indeed, there is evidence that growing numbers of students are letting computers overwhelm their lives, and concern over this issue is spreading.

The risk of this problem appears to be highest when students enter college. Some students go overboard, allowing computing to become their only way to connect to the world. Linda Tipton, a counselor at the University of Maryland, agrees that such problems are widespread, particularly among younger students beginning their college experience. Although the University of Maryland issues "computer accounts" to its students and limits them to 40 hours per week on campus terminals, some students spend more than six hours each day online. Many students feel most comfortable expressing themselves in a computerized setting.

Children and teenagers can benefit from being online, but they can also be targets of exploitation and/or deceit in this as in any other environment. Trusting, curious, and eager to explore this new world and the relationships it brings, children need parental supervision and common sense advice on how to be sure that their experiences in cyberspace are happy, healthy and productive.

In many ways, what happens online is just a bigger, electronic version of everyday life in the city or around the world. People come together to share ideas, make new friends, learn new things and conduct personal and professional business. And with new sites and new features being created every day, there is always something new to do or explore.

Real world

For parents, the same general skills that apply to the "real world" also apply to family computing. The best way to be assured that your children are having positive online experiences is to stay in touch with what they are doing. One way to do this is to spend time with your children while they're online. Have them show you what they do and ask them to tutor you on how to access the services. Consider taking advantage of the growing number of hands-on computing classes being offered by area schools.

Instead of attempting to control what your child experiences online, parents should actively participate with their children in online exploration. In fact, many experts specifically discourage the use of restrictive technology, urging instead that family computer use be based on simple, old-fashioned trust. "It is critically important for parents to recognize that children possess some basic rights in the digital age," writes computer expert Jon Katz. "If parents turn over responsibility to the Net Nanny, secure in the belief that it will do the work they should be doing, count on this: Children, many of whom helped build the digital culture, will swiftly transcend this software. They would be much better off if parents accompanied them when they first set out online, showing them what is inappropriate or dangerous."

Time

If you're worried that your child is showing signs of becoming obsessed with computing, a common sense approach works best. "The truth is," writes Judy Salpeter in *Kids and Computers*, "certain children during certain periods of their life will indeed become 'hooked' on computer activities, working on them at every free moment of the day." There's no such thing as 'the right amount of time' at the computer, but as with almost any activity that your child loves, you may need to encourage moderation."

Encourage your child to participate in group computer activities instead of engaging in purely solo computer time. Also, consider setting time limits at the computer. The American Academy of Pediatrics recommends no more than two hours of total media time per day, including TV, video games and computers. Any more than this means that kids are displacing essential hours of homework, physical activity, socializing time with friends and family, and hands-on learning in more experiential ways.

Games

With respect to computer games and software choices, adult ambivalence toward the electronic presence in children's lives is the "villain," according to media and child-development experts. When parents prefer not to examine what their children are watching or playing, or, when their attitude is that children's features are not worthy of adult attention, they are leaving their children alone in a grown-up environment.

Explore computer games with your child. "The good stuff is fantastic," says Peggy Charren, founder of Action for Children's Television. "The secret is to help the child get connected to what's wonderful…to mediate the stuff that isn't quite so good, and to say no to what's really awful." This may require research and a consensus on which programs to purchase.

In addition to seeking advice from professionals and publications, parents can also listen to their children, who seem to know intuitively about the best new software. Keep in mind that your child's willingness to try whatever you bring home will change dramatically as he gets older. Intellectually nutritious titles, based on art history or science, are not "cool" to older kids, who insist on an engaging setting, quick start-up, and lots of action. A good rule of thumb for parents is: involve your children in the buying decision.

Some families find it helpful for everyone to make a financial contribution to family software. The parents might contribute 50 percent of the cost of a program, big sister might pay 35 percent, little brother 15 percent, and so on. With everyone in the family agreeing on the purchase and providing at least some of the cost, the software will definitely be viewed as an item to be shared.

The whole family

Stop thinking that a computer is only for the kids! Reconsider your PC's location. For example, placing it in one child's room is not likely to encourage sharing, much less group participation. "The single most effective action you will take as a parent to control the computer is to put it in a common place," writes Matt Carlson, author of *Childproof Internet: A Parent's Guide to Safe and Secure Online Access*. Install the PC in a central location, such as a family room, where everyone has access to it. Such a public location limits where a child will go and allows parents to react to what appears on the screen.

Parents can take the time to show their children how they use the computer at work by retrieving office e-mail from home and letting them see what kinds of messages must be dealt with. Begin tracking family investments online, and enlist your children to look up the latest quotes or plot the daily highs and lows in a spreadsheet program.

The possibilities for involvement with your kids are endless. One idea Carlson practices regularly with his wife and children is "Family Night Online." One evening every two weeks or so is designated as a family night, with one family member assigned the responsibility of being the leader and setting the theme. "You will be amazed at what your kids come up with," says Carlson. "Whoever's the leader goes online in advance in order to research the theme, find related Web sites and set 'bookmarks' so that when we all gather round the computer, there's already a starting point to work from." There's no limit to the number of topics families can explore together; on given Family Nights the Carlsons have shopped for a new car, investigated colleges, tracked stocks and set up a portfolio, and planned vacations.

Even as we embrace the benefits of technology for the whole family, we must tell our children and ourselves that real knowledge comes from reading. Because so much published material is copyrighted it is therefore not available on the Web. Our electronic-age kids need to be reminded often that a vast store of knowledge is in the library.

Surfing safety

One of a parent's biggest concerns about the Internet is the proliferation of materials and sites inappropriate for children. For years parents have taught their children how to avoid strangers, and instilled values that steer them away from trouble. To the extent that this works in the real world, it seems logical to think that this approach may be transferred into the world of cyberspace.

Many Internet Service Providers (ISP) include parental controls in their online features and make them available to all subscribers. Typically, these controls allow parents to limit children's access to certain parts of the service or Internet sites. Many services also let parents set up logs to monitor where their children have spent their time online. In addition, most consumer online services have specially designated areas for children.

The online industry is working with a leading worldwide standards group to develop a voluntary system for rating online content. Known as the Platform for Internet Content Selection, (PICS), the system will allow groups to develop content ratings similar to the U.S. motion picture industry system for rating movies. Stay tuned.

Parents may choose to deal with the issue of inappropriate content on the Internet by using "parental control software." With names such as Cyber Patrol, Cybersitter, Surfwatch, and Net Nanny, these products steer young users clear of their own list of off limits places. The best can be updated periodically via the Internet. These software packages recently were rated in *Consumer Reports*, and the results indicate that none is totally effective since the Web changes too swiftly for even a full-time staff to maintain a complete list of adult sites. Also, their respective standards may not be in sync with yours, and overriding the software manufacturer's choices may not be possible. Finally, the blocking software may not work with your PC's online service.

Rules

Working together, families need to establish rules for computer use, just as there are rules for driving the family car. These rules should include where your child can go (yes or no to chat rooms, Usenet news groups, and so on), what your child can do (yes or no to sending e-mail messages, filling out online surveys, entering contests, etc.), and an understanding that some behavior is strictly off-limits. Many families have found it useful to post their agreed-upon guidelines near the computer. Some basic rules, noted below, provide families with a good starting point.

While children and teenagers need a certain amount of privacy, they also need parental involvement and supervision in their daily lives. If you have cause for concern about your children's online activities, talk to them. Also seek out the advice and counsel of other computer users in your local area and become familiar with the plethora of literature on these topics. Open communication with your children, utilization of available resources, and getting online yourself will help you obtain the full benefits of this exciting technology.

Kid's Own Rules for Online Safety

- I will not give out personal information such as my address, telephone number, parent's work address/telephone number, the name and location of my school, dance studio or athletic team without my parent's permission.
- I will tell my parents right away if I come across any information that makes me feel uncomfortable.
- I will never agree to get together with someone I "meet" online without first checking with my parents. If my parents agree to the meeting, I will be sure that it is in a public place and bring my mother or father along.
- I will never send a person my picture or anything else without first checking with my parents.
- I will not respond to any messages that are mean or in any way make me feel uncomfortable. It is not my fault if I get a message like that. If I do, I will tell my parents right away so that they can contact the online service.
- I will talk with my parents so that we can set up rules for going online. We will decide upon the time of day that I can be online, the length of time I can be online, and appropriate areas for me to visit. I will not access other areas or break these rules without their permission.

(Published by the National Center for Missing and Exploited Children)

See also: Cheating, Communicating, Dating, Harassment, Media

RESOURCES

Increasingly, area school and recreation centers are offering computer classes just for parents. Locating useful Web sites, learning how to use e-mail, and online services such as Netscape and America Online are topics presented during these hands-on tutorials.

Many monthly magazines are devoted to family issues relating to computer technology. They describe the latest technologies in easy-to-understand language and rate the best new hardware, software and peripheral products for family use. They even search the Internet to identify and list the best Web sites for parents and children of all ages. *Family PC* and *Family Circle's PC World* are only two examples.

Childproof Internet: A Parent's Guide to Safe and Secure Online Access, Matt Carlson, MIS Press, 1996.

"My Rules for Online Safety" is from a booklet titled *Child Safety on the Information Highway,* jointly produced by the National Center for Missing and Exploited Children and the Interactive Services Association, and written by Lawrence J. Magid. It is sponsored by America Online, CompuServe, Delphi Internet, e-world, Genie, Interchange Online Network and Prodigy.

A Student's Guide to the Internet: Exploring the Worldwide Web, Gopherspace, Electronic Mail and More! Elizabeth L. Marshall, The Millbrook Press, 1996.

Dating: Twos & Groups

When David was in the 5th grade, a 6th grade girl, Dana, called him to ask if he would "go with her." David put her on hold and went to talk to his mother. His mom said, "Tell her you'd be glad to be her friend but you don't want to go with anyone now, that you're only ten years old, and that your mother won't let you". He repeated all these reasons to Dana. She said, "OK, thanks, I'll call somebody else!"

Another approach might be for David's mom to ask him what "going" with someone meant. One 5th grader airily responded, "Oh, Mom, you just say you're 'going' with the person. What else would you do?"

Young adolescents need friendships with the opposite sex, and when adults view all boy-girl issues as romantic, they push children into dating before they are ready. Children as young as 11 or 12 may announce they are "going with" someone, but they are merely looking for the security of knowing "someone likes me." The same-sex friendships that dominate preteens' lives allow them to develop skills such as sharing emotions and learning give and take–skills that come into play in later dating relationships–without social or sexual pressure. According to David Elkind, Ph.D., "If children this age spend too much time in opposite sex relationships, they don't get to hone these skills."

Too young to date?

Today there are a lot of people who seem to think that earlier is better, whether it's toilet-training, walking, talking or dating. Early dating, particularly when older boys ask out younger girls, can make an already difficult period even more precarious. "Putting the brakes on preteen dating is something virtually every expert endorses. For kids ages 10-13, dating is developmentally inappropriate," says Karen Zager, Ph.D., a developmental psychologist. "It's like trying to drive an 18-wheel truck before you even know how to drive a car. There's too much information and too many complicated feelings for kids that age to integrate." But an adult's definition of dating may be quite different than a child's. For example, a group of boys and girls going to the movies or bowling together may go a long way toward promoting positive opposite-sex interactions without unnecessary "grown-up" stereotypes.

Kids this age are exposed to much more "mature" material on TV and in the movies than kids were a generation ago. Today, the message of the media as well as from peers, is that kids need a steady boyfriend/girlfriend to be accepted or okay. There may also be a more subtle source of pressure–parents themselves. Some parents have organized dances for elementary age children, describing their preteen dating rituals as "cute," while most children view these events with nervousness.

Define dating with your preteen

If our preteens want to date, our response should depend on whether or not we feel comfortable with what that means among their peers. Does it mean seeing each other weekends or after school? Do they go to movies, video arcades or skating rinks? Do they go alone, in groups or with other couples? Sometimes their outings resemble traditional dates, but usually preteen dating is far more innocent and informal. Sometimes kids who call each other boyfriend or girlfriend don't spend much time together, even on the phone.

If our preteen wants to be alone with his girlfriend, we can say, "You're not ready for this. Someday you will be, but not yet. Just as you're too young to drive a car, there are some things you can't do until you're older." Younger children often want to mimic what older kids do. The activities of older kids seem more exciting and give young children a chance to feel "grown up." If we give our children more freedom than they can handle–when we let them reach beyond their years–we set them up to fail.

We can offer compromises or alternatives. If we are comfortable with our preteen daughter talking on the phone with her boyfriend but don't want them going to a movie together, we can suggest an alternative suited to their age such as going to a sporting event or amusement park. If our child is among a coed group going to a movie, keeping the event confined to one place with an adult present at the beginning and the end may be most comfortable for all concerned.

Dating as teens

Dating is a brand new adventure for parents and teens alike. The age at which adolescents are ready to date varies from teen to teen. If we have given our children a solid foundation of our family's values, our son or daughter will know when that time is really right, rather than having peer pressure be the only reason behind the dating game. As parents, we should be available to offer reassurance and assistance to a child who may not be ready.

While most experts agree that teens are generally not ready for paired dating until the ages of 15-16 for girls and 16-17 for boys–that's where the application of many of the "traditional rules" end. Coed group outings and activities in middle school and high school have become a common way to explore changing interpersonal interactions. Paired dating still exists in high school, but it appears to be more intermittent and less intense than the dating most parents grew up with. It is not uncommon for friends to become romantically involved for a while and then go back to being just friends.

While dating has changed in its dimensions, it remains one of the primary mechanisms teenagers use to explore romantic feelings and develop the interpersonal skills necessary to ensure later success in long-term relationships. Notes Dr. Peter Spevak, Director of the Center for Applied Motivation in Rockville, "Besides fun, clear communication is one of the most important elements in dating. This includes communication between parents and adolescents about dating and...between dating partners." What teenagers know about communication and interpersonal relationships is first learned by observing and participating in family relationships throughout their early development.

Setting guidelines

"Sweet sixteen" is not a bad guideline for one-to-one dating. Group dating before this age may be reasonable, but even then we can give our children some guidelines. While providing them with support and protection, we can also recognize their increasing independence. We might explain, "I know you are growing up, and I want you to be independent and to enjoy yourself. But it's my job to help you make decisions that won't be harmful to you or to anybody else." We can then discuss why it is important for us to know who is going, where they are going, who is driving and when they'll be home. If we do not agree with these arrangements, further discussion is in order. If we have made a practice of letting our children know our plans when we're not home, asking the same of them will seem appropriate.

According to Dr. John Crocitto, middle-school counselor, it is advisable that dates be no more than two years older than your child. Fourteen-year-old Katie fell for a boy of eighteen. Katie made good grades and had been easy to parent, and the boy was a really decent guy. But dating someone so much older meant he would have to behave like a 14-year-old or Katie would have to behave like an 18-year-old, with all the responsibilities and privileges that entails. Even though Katie was a responsible child, she didn't have the experience and maturity to handle things on an 18-year-old level. Katie wasn't allowed to date the boy, but he spent occasional evenings with her family and they remained friends for years.

There are many steps we parents can take to help guide our children through the dating game. We can set reasonable curfews, allowing for a later evening for a special occasion. We can wait up or require our kids to wake us up when they get home. Middle and high school students should never attend unchaperoned parties; we always need to obtain the host parents' names, address, and phone number. Although it may be uncomfortable, it is important to call ahead to verify the occasion and ask questions about supervision and alcohol/drug policy. The initial premise for the phone call may be to thank the hosts and offer any support for the event. It's amazing how many parties are suddenly canceled when unsuspecting parents realize "they" are hosting a party while they are out of town!

When it's true love?

Jeannette had been dating Bob, who was three years older, ever since she was 16. Her parents objected because Bob had been in trouble with the law, had introduced Jeannette to drugs and alcohol, and had been the source of many unhappy hours for their daughter. On several occasions, Jeannette's parents had forbidden her to see Bob, only to discover later that she sneaked out and met him on the sly. They made their objections clear, pointing out Bob's weaknesses and faults, and threatened Jeannette with restriction and punishments for continuing to see him. When Bob phoned, they said Jeannette wasn't home; when he came over, they treated him coldly; they never included him in family celebrations.

When Jeannette graduated from high school, she ran away with Bob and got married. Two years later they were divorced.

As parents we need to exercise wisdom, good judgment and understanding. We can best do this by helping our children "work through" their needs. Jeannette needed to know more about what kind of person Bob really was. Her parents could have had her spend more time with Bob in their home; then Jeannette might have seen his negative side herself. It is fine for parents to express their concerns and doubts, but this must be done in a way that prevents the child's defensiveness and determination to prove them wrong.

"Going steady" should be discouraged. Unfortunately, some adolescents who are uneasy "playing the field," need more exclusive attachments. "Going steady" limits an adolescent's options and greatly increases the likelihood of sexual intimacy. Teen years on through college are a good time for meeting and dating lots of people. Teenagers are then better able to decide what kind of person they are most comfortable with.

What can parents do?

- *Establish an atmosphere where anything can be discussed* in a nonjudgmental manner.
- *Be available and encourage conversation.* While teenagers might try to push us away, they very much need and want the wisdom of our experience and guidance.
- *Include teenagers when developing rules* about curfews, driving, paired or group dates, so that they will understand the need for these limits.
- *Help your teenagers explore issues about relationships* including what

to expect, how to decide what they want out of a relationship, what is negotiable and what is not, and how to talk about things without being threatened or self-centered.

- *Share our own stories about early dating experiences* (as appropriate). Review our own approach to interpersonal relationships. Parental relationships are the first and most influential models for teenagers. Talk about a special occasion, such as a prom, or talk about an embarrassing time, such as spilling pizza in your date's lap. Then discuss how the situations were handled and what the results were. By sharing our faults, we give our children permission to learn from their mistakes.

What our children should know before dating

- *Communicate well with your date.* Be clear about significant likes and dislikes, your principles and values; be able to listen to each other in a nonjudgmental manner.
- *Recognize which areas are negotiable and which are not.* Three are non-negotiable: physical safety, the extent, if any, of physical intimacy, and issues involving drugs and alcohol.
- *Make decisions in advance.* Where are you going? Who are you going with? What are you going to do? Who's going to pay? Who's going to drive? Who else will be there?

Our teenagers need support, love and understanding. If these are absent at home, they will seek them elsewhere and lean heavily on anyone who has them to give. When children learn from their mistakes, they grow. If we make communication comfortable, keep our expectations clear, and are willing to compromise, our children's mistakes will not seem so drastic. Both our children and we will learn from our experiences.

See also: Date Rape, Driving, Parties, Sexual Responsibility

Date Rape

Statistics vary, but all of them are grim. It has been estimated that as many as one of every eight females in this country has been raped. More than 60 percent of rape victims are below the age of eighteen. One study predicts that one in four female college students will be the victim of a rape or an attempted rape during her college years, most likely during her freshman year.

The proverbial demented stranger leaping out of the bushes to grab a victim is not the reality behind these numbers. Most women and especially young women are raped by someone they know. In one study, 92 percent of adolescent rape victims knew their attackers. Unwanted sexual intercourse coerced by physical force or threats by someone the victim knows has been termed "acquaintance rape." "Date rape" is acquaintance rape by a social friend or in a social setting. Our children need to understand this phenomenon. Our daughters need to know how to minimize their risks and our sons need to know that we will not tolerate such behavior.

It's about boys *and* girls

Experts agree that rape is not primarily an act of passion. It is an act of domination and control. In the dating context, miscommunication between the sexes on the highly charged issue of sexuality is common and dangerous. Traditionally, boys have been encouraged to be aggressive and to actively go after what they want, in sports and otherwise. Society's traditional definition of masculinity encourages them to be proud of strong sexual feelings, to compete with their peers in making "conquests," and generally to appear "in charge" at all times.

Girls, on the other hand, are often encouraged to be more passive, to please, to be peacemakers and above all else to avoid making a scene. Often, girls are schooled not to appear eager for sexual activity, to avoid being labeled "loose." On the other hand, getting and keeping a boyfriend is highly prized in their world. In a climate where all young people are bombarded with a glamorous view of human sexuality through music, videos and movies–a sexuality often portrayed as accompanied with violence–it is hardly surprising that a few young men would interpret a young woman's less-than-forceful "no" as really a coy "yes," and feel it appropriate to "take charge."

Acquaintance rape can never be excused. Date rape is an illegal act, with very serious criminal and civil penalties. Its effects on young women can be devastating. Most victims of date rape suffer severe emotional consequences–including a crippling condition called post-traumatic stress disorder, the same affliction suffered by those returning from war or surviving other life-threatening events. At the minimum, date rape victims report a decline in their ability to trust others and to enjoy normal social and dating experiences.

What can we do to prepare our children?

First, experts agree that the best protection is a well-developed sense of self-esteem. The girl or young woman who has a secure sense of herself and her worth will not send out a message of vulnerability or doubt about her intentions. She will know her wishes and will be as assertive as she needs to be in order to communicate them. She will not need the approval of each of her dates in order to feel good about herself. A young man who believes in his own worth will not feel pressure to control a dating situation or to add a trophy to his collection. He will not need to "score," and will be interested only in a truly willing partner. We as parents can by word and deed support the values of independence and true self-love that will make our children's path in life easier.

Second, we can help our children be secure in their own values and decisions about sexual behavior and help them develop a strong respect for others, including others of the opposite sex. Parents may share their own values about pre-marital sexual activity, and listen with respect to the values developing in their children as they mature. They can talk to their children about the need to communicate clearly one's intentions in the area of sexuality, as well as the need to listen with care to the intentions of others.

Helpful strategies and observations for avoiding date rape

- Parents can counsel the wisdom of avoiding behaviors and situations that increase the likelihood of date rape.

- Parents can support their teens by providing an atmosphere that promotes healthy group activities for friends of both sexes. It is wise for a young woman to get to know a date well at home with her family, in a group situation or in a public place before being alone together in an isolated or secluded environment. Encourage group social activities whenever possible for all ages.

- Parents can counsel their children on the impact and illegality of alcohol and other drugs—which are often a significant factor in date rape. They can lower inhibition, increase aggressiveness and diminish a victim's awareness of warning signs that trouble is on the way. There have been increasing reports of the use of strong tranquilizers and amnesia-producing illegal drugs such as Rohypnol and GHB which have been slipped into drinks to lower or eliminate girls' resistance to sexual overtures.

- Parents can talk with their teens about the danger of mixed signals. Young women should think about whether their dress or the manner in which they present themselves could lead to miscommunication about their sexual attitudes. While excessive flirting, off-color joking or provocative dress never justifies date rape, it may be easier to moderate behavior in these areas to avoid raising erroneous expectations.

- Parents can help young persons of both sexes understand in their own minds what kinds of dating relationships they are seeking. Misunderstandings can arise when one party or the other is conflicted and sends out confused signals during a date. Once a young person understands his or her own wants and expectations, she can practice stating those intentions clearly, and taking care to understand the expectations of others before any sexual activity begins.

- Young women should know that they are supported in being "unpleasant" or even in making a scene, if necessary, when their instincts suggest that trouble is ahead. They should plan ahead, with parental support, to be able to leave any situation that becomes uncomfortable. For example, any teen feeling suddenly and inexplicably dizzy or ill at a party should feel comfortable calling her parents or 911 rather than accept "help" from her date.

- Parents need to be sure their sons know they can be prosecuted for acquaintance rape and that they do not believe that a woman should ever have to tolerate unwanted sexual behavior from anyone–including their son.

Get help immediately

Our daughters need to understand that they should seek personal support and professional and medical help as soon as possible following a rape or even an attempted rape. Explain to your daughter the urgent need for medical personnel to collect secretions and semen to validate the assault and to check for sexually transmitted diseases. Too often, date rapes go unreported to anyone, leaving the victim without a source of support at a most vulnerable time. Parents can discuss the option of aggressively seeking legal sanctions if their daughter is date-raped. While pressing charges against a person you know is incredibly difficult, rape is a criminal act.

Most communities have rape or crisis hotlines that can put a victim in touch with a trained counselor. For example, the D.C. Rape Crisis Center offers rape survivors thirteen and older a free three to four month course of individual counseling, together with group therapy if desired.

It is vital that parents offer unconditional love, comfort and support and never express the view that the victim "must have done something to ask for it"–greatly increasing a victim's trauma. Date rape victims need support as victims and not blame as collaborators in their own rape.

The books and article listed below as resources provide lists of specific dos and don'ts in the event a sexual assault should occur. In brief, it is best to act as quickly and aggressively as possible to extricate oneself from the situation. Pleading and crying are rarely effective.

See also: Alcohol, Alone, Clubs, Dating, Harassment, Parties

RESOURCES

A Guide to Rape Awareness and Prevention, R&J Ferguson. Turtle Press, 1994.

"'Friends' Raping Friends—Could It Happen to You?" J. Hughes & B. Sandler. April 1987, found at http://www.es.utk.edu/~bartley/acquaint/ acquaintRape.html

A Life Without Fear, L. Martin. Rutledge Hill Press, 1992.

I Never Called It Rape: The Ms. Report on Recognizing, Fighting and Surviving Date and Acquaintance Rape, R. Warshaw. Harper & Row, 1988.

Local Crisis Centers

DC: D.C. Rape Crisis Center 202 232-0789

MD:

Montgomery County Victim Assistance and Sexual Assault Services 301-217-1355

Prince George's County Sexual Assault Center 301-618-3154

VA:

Alexandria Sexual Assault Response and Awareness Program (SARA) 703-838-5030

Arlington County Victims of Violence Program 703-358-5150

Fairfax County Victims Assistance Hotline 703-360-7273

Depression: When Is It Over the Edge?

Every parent of a teenager can tell war stories about how adolescence distorted their charming, capable and cooperative child. Little girls who were once angels in tutus suddenly turn into door-slamming, telephone-hogging tyrants. Boys who were once funny and conversational, shun their families in favor of their friends and seem to have little to say. They stay out too late, may begin drinking and taking drugs. Some starve themselves; others become hopelessly sad and depressed, or ride a wild roller coaster between exhilarating highs and incapacitating lows. A few may try suicide, and sadly, some succeed.

Dr. Adelaide Robb, Medical Director of the Adolescent Inpatient Unit in the Department of Psychiatry and Behavioral Services at Children's National Medical Center, sees hundreds of troubled adolescents each year. She says the most critical element is knowing your child and establishing a baseline of what's normal.

"For a child who has always been a little irritable and rebellious, green hair is probably just the next step on a bumpy passage through life. But when somebody's adolescent rebellion interferes with his or her occupation—which is as far as I'm concerned, going to school and socializing— then that's bad. So, if somebody has green hair and is flunking out of school and has no friends, they're depressed. If they have green hair, but they're making straight As and everybody likes them, then they just have green hair."

Only about one percent of children who have not reached puberty become depressed, according to a report in the *Journal of International Pediatrics*, but eventually about 12.5 percent of all men and 25 percent of all women will suffer at least one episode of serious depression. At any given time, experts say, about one-fifth of the population is depressed. Forty percent of all adolescents who suffer from depression are at risk of serious depression again when they reach adulthood.

Many teens feel depressed

A survey of area teenagers done for *The Washington Post* in 1995 found that while 93 percent of both boys and girls said that they were generally happy, about a third of all the boys and more than half of all the girls said they often felt depressed or sad. About half of all teenagers said there was a lot of stress in their lives.

How can parents tell the difference between normal teenage rebellion and behavior that may indicate the onset of depression? Parents need to be particularly aware of eating behaviors, mood changes that could indicate the beginning of either depression or mania and, of course, incidences of alcohol or drug abuse.

Warning signs:

- A family history of depressive or manic/depressive personality disorders
- Changes in sleeping and eating habits or a noticeable weight loss or gain
- Feelings of excessive guilt, hopelessness or sadness
- Withdrawal from friends, family and regular activities
- A sudden drop in school performance, persistent boredom or difficulty concentrating
- Complaints of stomachaches, headaches, fatigue or other physical symptoms when no cause can be found, or a change in activity such as slowed movements, monotonous speech or unexplained agitation, such as fidgeting, pacing or wringing of hands
- Violent actions, rebellious behavior and running away
- Unusual neglect of appearance or a perception of being ugly

Risky behaviors

Dr. Robb explains that the most common form of depression among adolescents takes the form of an eating disorder, usually anorexia or bulimia. Although girls are generally more susceptible to eating disorders, about 1 in 10 cases do involve boys. "When you see a boy and he's growing taller and losing lots of weight, you might think that it's just because he's getting taller. But with boys, it's generally that they cut out fats and start exercising and lose lots and lots of weight. It's actually a form of anorexia," Dr. Robb notes. Parents should be especially watchful if their children are in "high-risk" activities including ballet, gymnastics, modern dance, ice skating, track and wrestling.

Mania is also fairly common among teens and is marked by either extreme happiness, extreme irritability or a very short fuse. "These kids generally have very rapid speech, or think grandiose thoughts or believe they have special powers that make them different from everyone else. They feel they are not answerable to normal social conventions or laws. In other words, they might think they can drive a car at 14 because they know how to drive a car. The fact that they don't have a driver's license or insurance doesn't stop them. They still want to take out the BMW and frequently, they get into serious trouble," she advises.

Finally, substance abuse–including alcohol and drugs–should be viewed much more critically. Juvenile use of alcohol and drugs is illegal, and is *not* a "normal part of growing up." "To get the money to buy drugs, most teenagers either steal from their parents or trade sex and that's not normal behavior. These children are drinking to excess and taking illicit drugs," Dr. Robb cautions. This behavior can lead to loss of money, loss of freedom (incarceration) and loss of life.

A predisposition or family history of depression can combine with other forms of stress and lead to depression. An episode of mononucleosis can trigger an onset of depression and so can drugs such as the steroids given to children who suffer from extreme cases of asthma. Beware of other potential stressors, such as the death of a friend or family member or even a beloved pet. Another significant stress point for some Jewish children is the bar or bat mitzvah. They're expected to achieve a level of proficiency and performance requiring a great deal of practice, in addition to their ongoing academic demands.

Too much stress

The pressure, particularly among children in Washington area schools, can be enormous and parents need to be especially concerned about how those stresses affect their children. When kids have setbacks, they can often feel that their problems are insurmountable. They may decide that no one understands them and that they are incapable of reversing their woes. When parents are unavailable to talk on a regular, daily basis, such depressive feelings can brew into a crisis.

"Parents must remember," Dr. Robb urges, "that teenagers haven't gone through a lot of failures or losses in life followed by future successes. If an adult loses a job or gets divorced, they can say, 'Well, I've had other jobs before and I'll find another one,' or, 'I had lots of boyfriends in high school and I can find another one, or just be by myself for while.' But teenagers, who don't have a lifetime of experience yet, only see the failure and become overwhelmed. A fatalistic thinking pattern combined with a lack of life experience precipitates illogical conclusions; even teenagers who are intellectually gifted don't always have those problem-solving skills," she notes.

Adult upheavals–financial, career, religious or marital stress–can have a profound effect on our children. Paradoxically, when our teens are beginning to experience their own inner churnings, they may be subjected to an environment of parental anxiety. Family changes, moving to a new house or a new school, and the acute rise in academic expectations of high school all put pressure on kids.

Parents need to know that help is available and that depression is treatable. The Washington area has a vast array of mental health services. If psychotherapy is recommended, parents need to be cautious in choosing a practitioner. Find out what kind of therapy is available–there are various methods and practices. Interview several candidates with your child (even as young as 10, a child will have a preference for one therapist over another). Get referrals from a trusted friend, family doctor, or guidance counselor. Social workers, psychologists, psychiatrists and counselors all have specialties and specific approaches. Don't hesitate to ask what they are, how your child would be seen (and how often), and how long the clinician has been in his or her speciality.

Because patient trust is crucial to the healing process, it's essential that you and your child feel you have made a "good match." Don't be discouraged if you don't find the "right one" on the first try; trust yourself and your child and stick with it. You have everything to gain and so much to lose.

See also: Alcohol, Eating, Loss, Stress

Driving

No matter how good it is, no driver's education program or commercial driving school alone can prepare your teen for driving on metropolitan Washington area's congested streets and highways. Parents need to play an active role in teaching their child how to drive. Norman E. Grimm, manager of traffic safety for AAA-Potomac, Fairfax, recommends that parents participate throughout the learning process and afterwards, and "not leave it up to the driving instructor."

Driving is far more dangerous today than it was when we parents learned to drive. Sharply increased congestion, complex traffic regulations and driving conditions, faster cars, more aggressive driving, higher numbers of elderly drivers and tourists unfamiliar with the area—these all add up to serious driving risk factors, according to Bud Nowland, owner of the Drive Right Driving School located in Gaithersburg.

Put an inexperienced young driver with the typical teenager's feeling of omnipotence behind the wheel of a 3,000 lb. vehicle that can accelerate from zero to 30 mph in seconds, and you've got all the ingredients for disaster, as these statistics from the National Highway Traffic Safety Administration (NHTSA) indicate:

- Motor vehicle crashes are the number one cause of death for teenagers in the U.S. Many who don't die are left permanently disabled or disfigured.

- During 1995, a young person (ages 15-20) died in a traffic crash an average of once an hour during weekends, and once every two hours on weekdays.

- Per mile driven, 16-year-old drivers have the highest rate of fatal crash involvement by a large margin. Seventeen-year-olds have the next highest rate.

Although alcohol-related fatalities have declined over the past ten years, alcohol remains a major factor in fatal accidents: 2,206 youths died in alcohol-related crashes in 1995.

Good drivers don't just happen

Experts suggest that a major reason so many young people are involved in accidents is that they are poorly trained. Help give your kids the tools they need to be safe on the road by taking an active part in their training. Here's how:

- *Model the behavior you want your teen to exhibit.* Children's behavior and attitudes are shaped when they're very small children. Learning how to be a good, safe driver doesn't happen when a child is 15-16 years old. It happens from the ages of 4-15 as he observes his parents' driving habits. Do you want your child to drive the way you do?

- *Learn (or relearn) the traffic regulations in your jurisdiction.* Chances are they've changed significantly since you first learned to drive. Make sure your knowledge is up-to-date so that you're prepared to advise your teen properly.

- *Brush up on proper driving methods.* Many of these have changed, too, since most of us learned to drive. For example, the recommended position for hands on the steering wheel is no longer at the traditional 10 and 2 o'clock position on the steering wheel, says Nowland. "AAA changed their recommendations about five years ago to 8 and 4 or 7 and 5," he notes.

- *Practice "commentary driving."* As teens near 16, help prepare them for their time behind the wheel by raising their awareness of all that goes into driving. "With the child in the front seat as you drive, talk about what you're seeing and thinking, and the decisions you make," Nowland suggests. Articulate all of the actions you take (and that you now do almost automatically) and describe the thought processes behind them. For example, "Even though the light in front of us is green, I see that pedestrian on the right starting to step off the sidewalk, so I've taken my foot completely off the accelerator. I am stepping on the brake to slow the car down until I know what she's going to do. Now that she has stepped back up on the curb, I've taken my foot off the brake and put it back on the accelerator so that I can get back up to speed."

Take an active role in training

Don't assume that driving is mandatory at age 16. Some parents want to make the 16th birthday a rite of passage that includes the right of a driver's license. But not everyone is ready to drive at age 16. Make the decision about your own child's readiness based on her maturity, kinesthetic and visual-coordination skills and attitude. Take a cue from your teen. She may feel peer pressure to drive, but may be apprehensive because she really does not feel ready to undertake that task. Reassure your teen that individual readiness varies greatly and that her time frame is something you two can judge best together.

Be realistic about how long it takes to become a skilled driver. Some experts suggest that teens spend 200-500 miles on the road with a parent in the car before being allowed to drive on their own. Make sure that kids get the training and practice they need before turning them loose, unsupervised, on the streets and highways. Even then, don't expect them to be expert drivers. AAA suggests that it takes three to five years to become a good driver.

Use a graduated approach to driving. "When children receive six hours of behind-the-wheel training, there's no way they can gain the experience they need" to be a safe driver, Grimm of AAA-Potomac reminds us. According to the Insurance Institute of Highway Safety, "A promising approach to the overall problem involves modifying 16-year-olds' initial driving, helping them learn by controlling pro-gressive to unrestricted driving, and lifting controls one by one until a young driver graduates to full licensure." In other words, easy does it.

If your jurisdiction has not adopted graduated licensing, you can take that approach by restricting your teen's driving while he gains the training and experience he needs to survive on today's roads. Parents can consider developing an approach based on the number of miles driven (for example, a teen must be accompanied by a par-ent until he has driven 200 miles), taking into consideration the types of road, weather, time of day, and traffic congestion. Nowland sug-gests a parent act as a driving coach, giving a teen experience on both country and city roads, highways, shopping centers, at night, and in various weather conditions. Have your teen drive in a parking lot when it snows and have him learn how to counteract skids.

Check out driving schools carefully. Use the AAA's brochure to investigate commercial driving schools carefully before you select one.

Establish rules for car use and maintenance. Be firm about your expectations regarding:

- Drinking, drug use and driving
- Your teens notifying you where they're going and when they'll return
- Number of passengers allowed in the car, if any, and their names (some parents require that any passengers have their parents' permission to ride in the car)
- Restrictions on car use (such as night time driving, highway or city driving, or during hazardous weather conditions)
- Driver's responsibility for reporting accidents and traffic violations
- Use of the car to run errands
- Consequences for not adhering to the rules you develop

Define your family's driving rules

Many experts recommend spelling out family driving rules especially regarding drinking, drug use and driving in a "safe-driving" contract that is signed by parents and the teen driver. AAA's "Vehicle Use and Operation Agreement" spells out the teen's possible responsibilities, including items they might be required to pay for (such as cost of fuel, insurance, registration, fines and penalties, collision damage, etc.), maintenance that the young driver may be responsible for (such as checking the fluids and tire pressure, cleaning windows, etc.), maximum number of miles driven per week (perhaps linked to grades in school), loss of privileges for traffic offenses and at-fault crashes, regulations that must be followed (such as seat belt use, whether or not to lend the car, no drugs or alcohol, etc.). Spell out the consequences. Consider offering incentives for good driving.

Establish a no-fault pickup policy whether your child is the driver or a passenger. Let your teen know you want him to call home for a ride or that you'll pay for a cab, no questions asked, any time they feel they should not drive home or should not be a passenger in a car driven by a peer.

Consider a car phone but be clear as to use. A cell or car phone makes it possible for your child to check in with you or contact you in case of an emergency, or if she gets lost. However, talking on the phone while driving can distract young and older drivers alike, so include phone use in your family driving rules.

Educate your child about the effects of alcohol on driving. According to AAA, young drivers with a blood alcohol concentration (BAC) equivalent to one to two drinks "are at least seven times more likely to be killed in a crash than a sober driver of any age," while a young driver with a BAC equivalent to three or four drinks "is 40 times more likely to be killed than a sober driver...."

More to consider

Take a hard look at the car your child will be driving. Consider how well the car will protect your teen driver in the event of an accident. Is it safe? Well-maintained? Equipped with important safety technology such as air bags and antilock brakes?

After your teen has a full license, ride with him occasionally to observe driving habits. From time to time, ask your child to give you a ride to the store, or drop you somewhere. Doing so will enable you to observe his driving skills (both good and bad). Use these opportunities to gently coach young drivers on good driving methods and decision-making long after they've gotten their license.

Consider the advantages of *not* buying a car for your teen. The major benefit is that not having regular access to a car limits your teen's driving, enabling her an opportunity to gradually gain experience.

Help kids learn their way around. Invest some time in familiarizing your teen driver with the major streets and highways they're likely to travel. Use local maps to give them the big picture, and introduce them to the way streets in your jurisdiction are laid out. Help them keep abreast of construction in the area, and to map out alternate routes they can use in the event of construction or traffic tie-ups. For trips to unfamiliar locations, write out clear directions and help your teen plot them on a map.

Make teenagers aware of their legal rights and responsibilities, such as what to do and say in the event of an accident (regardless of who is at fault) or if they're stopped by the police.

Make the use of seat belts and motorcycle helmets (they are required by law) mandatory. According to the NHTSA, of the 1,135 18-year-old occupants of passenger vehicles who died in 1995, 744 or 65 percent were not wearing safety belts. Make buckling up a must for drivers and passengers.

Passengers at risk

Being a driver is not the only thing that's hazardous for teens. Passengers are at risk, too. Just being a passenger can be fatal. According to NHTSA, youths aged 15-20 account for almost one-fourth of all passenger fatalities. Know your children's drivers. Make sure that they have the same levels of experience and expertise that you expect your own child to have. Establish a code phrase that your teen can use to call you to request a ride whenever he is concerned about a peer's ability to drive.

See also: Alcohol, Communicating, Risky Business

RESOURCES

Publications from the AAA include brochures on "Alcohol, Vision and Drinking," "One Drink Can Be Too Many," "Choosing a Driving School," plus "Teaching Your Teen to Drive: A Partnership for Survival," which includes a handbook and video or CD-Rom. Available from AAA-Potomac, 703-222-4104.

Safe Young Drivers: A Guide for Parents and Teens, Phil Berardelli, EPM Publications Inc. This spiral-bound book, written and published locally, is designed to be read by parents and teens alike. A valuable guide while preparing for the drivers' test, it is also a quick reference to be kept in the car afterwards. 703-442-7810 (mention The Parents Council of Washington for discounted price).

Organizations

Mothers against Drunk Driving, (MADD) National Office, 214-744-6233, http//:www.madd.org

Students against Drunk Driving, (SADD) National Office, 508-481-3568

Eating Healthy & Harmful

Food provides the essential elements of fuel and social sharing. It is important that families find opportunities to be together, to eat together and to stay connected.

Family rituals involving food go beyond traditional holiday events. They can include everything from sharing breakfast with the child you commute with to having dinner each evening at a certain time or at whatever time the family can manage to find together. Other opportunities for sharing range from once a week at a restaurant of a family member's choice, Wednesday evening dinner chosen and cooked by one child, group consensus on occasional carry-in dinners, etc. Create opportunities where you dine as a family and establish the companionship of eating.

Our bodies depend on the food we put into them for energy, growth and maintaining normal daily health. It is sometimes difficult to determine if our children are eating the right things in the correct amounts at the right times and if they have a healthy relationship with food. After all, much of what is eaten by our children is consumed out of our view when they are in school, with friends, or home alone. Growing children have varying nutritional needs as they go through growth spurts, change their activity level, develop food preferences, and mature. Children should know that bodies change over time, especially during the teen years. Parents should, to the best of their ability, be aware of what their children are eating.

According to Ellyn Satter, M.S., R.D., author of *How to Get Your Child to Eat...But Not Too Much,* a parent's responsibility is to provide regular, healthy meals and to make mealtime a pleasant occasion. Put enough food on the table and let your child help decide what and how much to eat. Setting rigid rules only leads to power struggles. What we put into out bodies is a highly individual decision. Our job as parents is to make those essential items available and appealing in a comfortable setting–physical as well as emotional.

Body image

How kids feel about their body shape and size is critical to their approach in eating. In this country there is almost a frenzied pathology to how we approach the process of influencing our naturally determined shape and size. There is still much we don't know about the impact of genetics, the environment and various other factors on how and how much we can influence our biologically predisposed shape and size. Changing or attempting to alter body shape and size is a multi-billion dollar business and accounts for much individual and collective cultural angst.

Girls as young as second and third grade feel the need to lose weight. One survey of kindergartners indicated that they believe it is worse to be fat than to be in a wheelchair. Diet mentality and chronic dieting put children at risk for developing eating disorders.

Diane Heim, Director of the Eating Disorders Program at Georgetown University Hospital, states, "Parents play a key role in helping to establish their child's body image. It is important to help children have a positive self-image *before* they are subjected to the influence of peer pressure in adolescence. Parents who give no feedback on how a child looks, only negative feedback, or too often emphasize beauty, are putting the child at risk."

Adolescents and young adults, especially females, are susceptible to additional pressures to achieve or maintain a particular look. The look that is currently held as the female ideal is one that is irrationally based on an anorexic driven modeling industry. The waif model (dramatically underweight) body type is only naturally achievable by 5–7 percent of the population and is, in fact, a generally unhealthy example. Parents have to help their children realize that not everyone has a "perfect body," nor is a perfect body the key to a happy life.

Sports nutrition

Every child and adolescent needs the same types of foods to fuel their bodies. Student athletes need greater amounts of nutrients to compensate for their high energy expenditure and additional fluids to counteract dehydration. Unfortunately, some sports also have additional pressures to be a certain weight or to look a certain way. Pressure from a coach to lose body weight or body fat can be significant for some sports. Sometimes there is a fine line between what could and should be done safely without putting a child at risk for developing eating problems.

Know where your coaches stand on dramatic weight loss for sports. Sports which carry the biggest risk are gymnastics, track, wrestling, ballet, swimming and diving. The coach may be correct that a child should reduce some body fat, but this should never be done quickly or dramatically. Some student athletes may try various techniques which place the body under significant stress such as laxatives, diet pills, "spitting," eliminating water or excessive exercise. None of these techniques is healthy or effective, and all are damaging to growing bodies. Consult a sports nutritionist or a sports medicine specialist for individual advice.

Talk with the coach and challenge her if you feel that excessive or unrealistic demands are being made–by the coach or your child. You know your child best, and you are his greatest advocate. Too often parents unwittingly collude with the coach and the sport in unhealthy standards. Remaining silent in the face of disturbing efforts to accomplish weight loss serves as a form of endorsement and can jeopardize your child's health and future.

Eating disorders

Sensible nutrition, moderate exercise, positive self-esteem and a supportive family offer the best prevention for obesity and eating disorders.

People with eating disorders spend a lot of time thinking about eating, food, weight and body image. They may count and recount calories in their meals, weigh themselves daily and place themselves on severely restricted diets regardless of their weight. They often "feel fat" when their weight is normal or abnormally low, or feel uncomfortable after consuming a normal sized or small meal. They may eat compulsively. Generally, they categorize food as "good" or "bad," and make judgments about themselves based on how well they control what they eat. Believing that others are also judging them based on their control of food, they frequently feel anxious eating in front of people.

Eating disorders are very complex diseases that involve physical, psychological, social, cultural, and familial components. Current theories about how one develops an eating disorder vary and include the following aspects: depression, feelings of inadequacy, troubled personal relationships, difficult major life events such as loss or transitions, and biochemical imbalances.

Warning Signs of an Eating Disorder

- Restrictive dieting
- Development of abnormal eating habits
- Feelings of isolation, depression or irritability
- Fat phobia–fear of fat grams
- Compulsive or excessive exercising
- Intense preoccupation with weight, obsessions with food and/or body image
- Increase or decrease in weight
- Emotional or compulsive eating
- Scars or marks on the index finger which result from forced vomiting

The following disorders are usually best treated by a multi-disciplinary team of health professionals.

Anorexia Nervosa

- Weight at less than 85 percent of that expected for height and bone structure
- Intense preoccupation with thinness and fear of gaining weight
- Distorted sense of body weight or shape

Bulimia Nervosa

- Recurrent episodes of binge-eating (eating an unusually large amount of food within a certain period of time while feeling out of control)
- Episodic purging behavior, including vomiting, use of laxatives; or fasting or excessive exercise to prevent weight gain

- Overconcern with body weight and shape
- Usually average or slightly above average weight

Binge Eating Disorder

- Binge eating with no purging
- Episodes of binge eating more than two times a week for a period of six months
- Usually above average weight

How to help

You can be part of the solution if you:

- Insist that your child get professional help
- Remain calm, unemotional and are honest in talking with your child about the situation, the behavior and its consequences
- Encourage new interests and include your child in activities that she enjoys
- Be patient as eating disorders take a long time to develop and recovery does not occur overnight. Try to accept setbacks and relapses with understanding and calmness.

You will make things more difficult if you:

- Ignore the situation
- Attempt to be controlling
- Argue about food

Prevention tips

- Develop an alliance with your children. Educate them about nutrition, sensible weight management and the dangers of eating disorders
- Model good eating habits
- Evaluate your own messages to your child about weight, dieting, beauty and body
- Tell your child that body shape or size is just a small part of who you are

- Talk about the media's influence on our images of the "right" body and how unrealistic TV and magazine portrayals are

- Talk to your child about the pressures people feel to lose weight, or be attractive

- Help your child define his own values and determine what's really important about himself

See also: Depression, Friendships, Harassment, Push for Success, Smoking, Stress

RESOURCES

American Anorexia/Bulimia Association, Inc., 212-575-6200

American Dietetics Association, 800-877-1600

Dominion Hospital, Eating Disorders Program, 2960 Sleepy Hollow Road, Falls Church, VA 703-538-2874

Georgetown University Hospital, Eating Disorders Program, 3800 Reservoir Road, N.W. Washington, DC, 202-687-5075 or 687-8609

International Association for Eating Disorders Professionals, 561-338-6494

National Association of Anorexia Nervosa and Associated Disorders, 847-831-3438

Friendships

A 9th-grader tearfully described to her mother how she felt she was a "loser." She wanted to be able to be relaxed with classmates, to hug friends and to laugh out-loud. Her mother knew that although her daughter was not "painfully shy," she did seem out of sync with her peers and often ill at ease with them.

Making friends is easier or harder based on our child's personality. The now famous research on temperament, the New York Longitudinal Study, conducted by Chess and Thomas beginning in the 1950s, identified distinct temperamental traits, including activity level, distractibility, intensity, persistence and adaptability. Most children—as well as adults—can be classified as "easy," "difficult" or "slow to warm." These natural, innate personality traits are our child's way of responding to the world around him, his characteristic disposition. Even as babies, some children are more hesitant in social situations, less comfortable to accept new people and need more time to warm up. Styles generally persist throughout one's life, so it's not surprising that some teens need more time to feel confident in a variety of social situations and with different peer groups.

Some children just don't seem to know how to make friends. This may be because they come from a household that is so self-contained that it has few friendships, other interests, and contacts beyond the family. Our children learn how to make and keep friends, at least in part, by watching us. If our home is one where friends seldom call and visitors seem unwelcome, our children may not develop the social skills needed to make friends.

Some shyness or social discomfort is biologically based; it is more likely that a shy child comes from at least one introverted parent. Parents who were shy as children, who felt lonely or excluded, may pressure their own children to become gregarious and popular. As parents we need to gently encourage our shy child, focusing on her strengths and never referring to her shyness in a derogatory manner or as an insurmountable impediment.

Shyness can also stem from low self-esteem due to learning disabilities or poor school performance that may cause a child to avoid social situations. Some socially inept children may suffer from "dyssemia," a recently discovered learning disability that interferes with the ability to properly decode and understand non-verbal cues and communication. Others may not be able to follow the subtleties of a conversation due to problems processing language. Whatever the cause, the impact of feeling "left out," can exacerbate undesirable behavior, compounding the situation.

Sometimes, cautions the faculty of Children's National Medical Center in *A to Z Guide to Your Child's Behavior*, preteens go through a shy period as they become more self-conscious and fearful of making mistakes in front of their peers. This is different from lifelong shyness and usually eases with the passage of time and empathetic conversations with parents. Research has shown that children can overcome formidable obstacles if they have the ability to form at least one intimate friendship with a peer or an adult.

Not easy for some

Not all teens find it easy to make friends. A very few are natural "loners," people who are so self-contained that they don't seem to need or want friends. But there are many more who do care, who feel like a failure, alone and unliked. Feeling friendless is a miserable state.

Most teenagers lack the maturity and experience to realize that success and popularity in high school have very little to do with how much success they will reap in the adult world. We have all known people who just don't seem cut out to be adolescents; they come into their own as adults. While this reality may provide very limited comfort to our teenager, it does allow us to be honestly hopeful and reassuring.

We all want our children to form successful social bonds and "fit in." Sometimes, this goal seems unattainable for unknown and inexplicable reasons. Then we suffer, too, of course. Especially when we feel helpless to improve our child's situation, we feel distress. During the preteen and teen years we are understandably reluctant to pick up the phone and discuss it with "other parents."

Our concern may well be sensed by our child, which only intensifies her sense of "failure." However, although we are very sociable and have many friends and social activities, our child may be content with a much slower pace and smaller numbers. If our child seems comfortable with his friendships, we may need to accept that he is a naturally shy person. The world needs both extroverts and introverts.

Sometimes we just need a "reality check." One parent, whose son had been bemoaning his lack of friends, was told by the child's advisor that at school he was always with a couple of classmates, was well regarded, and was frequently seen chatting and laughing with peers. It turns out that he had friends; he just didn't feel he had much of a social life–a not uncommon reality for teenagers (especially boys) who seem to find it difficult to get organized to "go out."

Whatever the explanation, children who feel left-out may give the impression of being aloof or unfriendly so that other teens hesitate to make the first move toward friendship. They need our help to connect with peers, to work out why friends are so hard for them to come by, and to improve their chances of making friends.

Cliques and bullies

Child development experts agree: cliques and bullies have always existed, making life miserable for the children who are different, less outgoing or socially insecure. Although common, especially in the middle school years, such occurrences can be devastating and are best monitored by school personnel as well as parents. Rejection can interfere with any child's education; instead of focusing on their studies, children may focus on their inadequacy and fear.

Being excluded, teased, threatened or called names–especially in front of others–erodes any child's self-confidence, but even more if the child is socially insecure. Adolescent standards can be very harsh–the teen who is considered too plain, quiet, or unathletic may fail to meet the current standards. When our child is the one picked on, we can listen, sympathize and advise her to not let the behavior hurt. All parents should talk with their children about bullies and kids who exclude others.

Parents of bullies or children who are in exclusionary cliques often don't recognize there is a problem since their child doesn't behave that way when they are around. However, we need to be sure our attitudes or behavior (such as praising our children for being tough or insisting that they be superior to or stronger or smarter than peers) don't encourage aggression. If our child is persistently bullying or excluding, it means he or she is deficient in her ability to interact socially and to think through behavior options. Without guidance our child may have long-term difficulties succeeding socially.

Friendliness can be learned

Social skills can be learned, and we can be part of the process. In fact, a parent may be the only one a child can approach with this issue, and we certainly are in the best position to recognize the need for development in these skills. Adolescent specialists encourage us to seek professional intervention for our children early; don't wait until her senior year to worry about whether she will have friends in college.

If the problem is with peer socializing, it may best be addressed in a group setting with professional guidance. Many area psychologists and language therapists specialize in helping the child who "doesn't fit in" with role play and other strategies. These services can be provided individually, but are best in small groups of similar-age children. In these sessions, children learn about communication–skills such as how to really listen, how to interject comments into an ongoing conversation, how to avoid inappropriate interruptions and comments, how to maintain eye contact, and avoid standing too close, and how to use phrases that redirect the conversation or change the subject. As parents we can reinforce the skills in family conversations, encourage even little successes, and assure our child that, little by little, he is improving.

We can also help our children recognize that while it's nice to be well-liked, popularity is fleeting. Popular teens may have lots of casual friends, but often few close friendships. Super-socializing teens may be sapping time from academics–a tremendous disadvantage in the years ahead. And we can remember aloud that the most enthusiastic participants in our high school reunions are often the ones who "peaked" in their teens.

While it is not always easy to take a hard look at our children and admit their weaknesses, if they are feeling friendless, we owe them some help. One study of popular versus rejected adolescents found that teens who were well-liked were described as cheerful, friendly, humorous, attractive, athletically able (especially the boys), and that they "suggested games and activities." Teens who were rejected were characterized as: restless, over-talkative, too quiet or shy, unattractive (especially too overweight), and "different."

We can help our teenagers recognize that while they can't change other people, they can try to change themselves. The first step is to help our children consider themselves from other people's perspective. Some possible questions for self-analysis are:

- Do you always wait for someone else to make the first move?
- Are you expecting exclusivity? Are you jealous if a friend socializes with someone else?
- Are you more critical than supportive of others?
- Can you be counted on as a friend?
- Do you feel inferior or disparage yourself?
- Do you offer help, even unsolicited help?
- Do you ever talk to kids who seem shy or alone?
- Do you try to see things from another's point of view (during an argument)?
- Are you a good listener? Do you tend to monopolize a conversation?
- Are you kind? If someone seems sad do you try to cheer them up?

Honest answers to these questions can reveal why making friends is so difficult. Considering these issues and deciding where changes might be made can improve our child's chances of making friends.

Advice and sensitivity

Almost all children feel left out at some point during their lives. All children need to feel unconditional love and support from their parents—especially when the rest of their world doesn't feel satisfying. As parents we can encourage discussions about feelings, listen empathically, avoid trivializing, and perhaps offer anecdotes of our own childhood experiences of not fitting in. We can:

- *Act as role models for our children* by inviting guests to our home, engaging in hobbies or activities with other adults, and participating in community or school events.

- *Stay "up to date" about our children's social situations and friends*; we will find it easier to know when our children are experiencing difficulties. If a child is not forthcoming, knowing the "key players" will allow us to ask the right questions.

- *Encourage our children to pursue their interests and skills.* Feeling competent enhances our children's feelings of self-worth, which in turn enhances their social skills.

- *Consider letting our child select a pet.* Pet ownership conveys responsibility and fosters expressions of intimacy and empathy that may transfer to peers and others.

- *Very discreetly discuss our child's shyness or social problems with his teachers and counselor.* Sometimes, a simple accommodation alone, such as seating a child with a prospective friend or assigning a special partner for a group project, can make an enormous difference. (Many schools are aware of the devastating consequences that can result from being excluded and have created conflict resolution and diversity training programs for the classroom. We can investigate what our school offers and what resources are available.)

Friendships you don't like

We can't dictate who our children will like, and trying to discourage a friendship may actually strength the attraction. Early adolescence begins the period when our children select friends who they feel help define their emerging identities. If we discourage friendships they have handpicked, they may perceive our action as criticism of them.

When we don't like our child's friend, we need to first ask ourselves, "What bothers me about this kid?" If we find that our reasons are basically superficial (such as hairstyle, language, clothing), a good tack is to try to ignore them and trust our child's judgment. If the other child is outlandish in some way, we can consider that our child may be using the friend to continue the separation process. This is a time when we may need to explore our own prejudices. Absent dangerous behavior, we can console ourselves that while peer influence may reveal itself in superficial ways, parental influence remains powerful in the most crucial areas.

Talking with our child about the behaviors or qualities which alarm us can underscore our family's views, beliefs and standards without openly criticizing those of the other child or her family. This situation is ideal to acknowledge (once again) to our children that saying "no" is not always easy–especially if she really enjoys the friend and wants to stay connected. If her identity is secure, she won't be so dependent on the approval of friends.

A frequent adolescent issue is peer pressure. If our child is vulnerable because he wants so badly to "belong," if he is persuaded to join a rough crowd or do something thoughtless, dangerous or illegal, then we do need to be concerned. Children who haven't received firm, positive direction from their parents and haven't established a strong connection to their family are most susceptible to negative friendships.

In continuing to stress compassion and concern for others, we can help our children develop empathy and understanding of different styles of social skills and needs. We should emphasize that words can wound. Our own attitudes and casual comments are signals to our children about what kinds of behavior we consider appropriate.

We need to monitor our children's friendships, even–perhaps especially–during the teen years. But we must remain respectful as well as aware. Our children benefit from knowing kids from different backgrounds and with different points of view. If we model having a diverse group of friends, our children can comfortably follow suit. Our overall acceptance of our child's friends indicates our overall acceptance of her in her growing social independence.

Worth(y) of friendship

A feeling of belonging to a community, of being part of a strong supportive network of family and friends, is one of the most important buffers our children can have against depression and peer pressure. At any age, our children need to exercise their own judgment in selecting their friends. This is part of the process of discovering their identity.

The child who is socially vulnerable needs a lot of support. If she doesn't get it from her parents, she probably won't get it. We must remind our children of their strengths, that they are worthy of love and friendship, and of our confidence that they will acquire the skills to overcome their difficulties.

See also: Depression, No!, Risky Business, Yes!

Gender: Raising Boys & Girls

What kind of women will our daughters become?
What kind of men will our sons be?

Parenting a child of either sex is a major job. We want our children to be themselves, to make their own decisions, to feel fulfilled, and to move beyond sexist and racist attitudes and behavior. Yet somehow it is easier to remember that we want Julia to be able to have the option of choosing to attend law school than that we want Joshua to learn household tasks.

Sexism is a two-edged sword, and boys as well as girls pay a price. David Sadker, American University professor and author of *Failing at Fairness,* explains, "The male stereotype includes greater risk-taking behavior, a higher suicide rate, and a greater involvement in criminal activities. In school, boys are more likely to need special education services, and they have a slightly higher dropout rate. The need to overcome society's sex-role stereotypes is as important to boys who dream of becoming teachers or nurses as it is to girls who dream of a career in electrical engineering. While girls lag behind on most critical standardized tests, boys continue to receive lower report card grades."

Because we aspire to what is possible, parents can ensure that their daughters as well as their sons see the future as flexible and filled with endless choices.

Raising girls

If our goal is to raise daughters who have the courage to speak their minds and the power to do what they believe in, we need to:

- Praise girls for their skills and successes, not only for their appearances. Say, "You did a terrific job," instead of "You look pretty today."

- Avoid rescuing girls. Encourage them to get dirty, disheveled and sweaty climbing trees or playing in the grass. Allow them to take risks.

- Debunk the myth of Prince Charming. Teach girls that most women will work for pay for most of their lives. Every girl needs to be prepared to support herself.

- Teach girls to watch TV– including the commercials–and movies with a critical eye. Discuss what you've seen together: Look for strong, smart women who are not limited to "traditional" roles.

- Use TV to start a discussion about body image. Consider how girls are portrayed on TV. Are heavier girls shown as unpopular? Do they go out on dates? Are they used as comic relief? Are girls with voluptuous figures only shown as sex symbols? Do they seem to be smart?

- Create opportunities for your daughter to challenge herself in areas where females have traditionally been "protected." For example, have her change the oil in the car, take apart a computer or rock-climb.

- Promote your daughter's physical and mental health, including preventing eating disorders, substance abuse, and violence against girls.

- Give girls more opportunities to be leaders. Let them choose the activity, make the rules, settle the dispute. A girl who has learned to lead is better prepared to take charge of her own education and career.

- Give girls many opportunities to experience science, math and technology.

- Help girls get beyond "yuk." Insist calmly that girls hold a snake, dissect a worm, get their hands dirty discovering the world around them.

- Introduce girls to dynamic women who combine paid work, volunteer work and family life.

- Be an example. By respecting yourself and other women, you set a standard for girls to follow.

- Emphasize to girls that computers can be an important tool for learning, networking and communication; they need to see its relevance to their lives.

Raising boys

If our goal is to raise sons who respect and support women, we need to:

- Foster your son's relational skills, such as his ability to nurture, empathize, sympathize and be compassionate. Provide opportunities for him to read to or care for younger children, the disabled or elderly. Pets also promote caring and nurturing skills.

- Foster your son's ability to feel strongly and to recognize those feelings: how to feel love, to neither discount fear nor be overwhelmed by it, and how to enjoy feeling deeply.

- Talk with your son about men who work in nontraditional roles such as stay-at-home dads, dancers and nurses.

- Acknowledge the pressures put on men in this society to prove themselves by appearing tough or exhibiting "machismo" and offer examples of alternative behaviors that do not mean men are weak or have no pride. In spite of traditional stereotypes, boys need to have the strength to define their masculinity in a way most comfortable to them. This kind of self-definition is a work in progress that we can allow to begin at home.

- Talk to boys about gender roles, attitudes about work, home life, fatherhood, mentors, and stereotypes of both men and women.

- Remember that many boys are themselves targets of sexual harassment—often in the form of taunts challenging their sexuality. This destructive behavior directed at boys is no more acceptable than sexual harassment directed at girls.

- Ensure that our sons see that gender equity is not giving up some thing—power, status, privilege—but about the addition of consciousness, building that old-fashioned thing called "character."

Raising people

Raising boys and girls, is really raising *people*—people who appreciate their innate uniqueness and worth. When boys and girls value their own strengths, they are more likely to appreciate those around them.

- Whether you have daughters or sons, share moments of spontaneous thrill to just be alive—chasing bubbles blown into the yard, stopping along the road to get out and gape at a rainbow. These are moments that transcend gender.

- Encourage your children and their peers to observe each others' behavior and to discuss gender-biased behavior when it occurs, especially when a peer says "that's for sissies," "girls can't do that," or "he throws like a girl."

- Raise kids' awareness of the ways gender bias can be transmitted. For example, work with your children to evaluate books, magazines, songs or toys for the degree of gender bias.

- Seeing men in nurturing and caregiving roles gives both our boys and girls permission to "own" these roles.

- Introduce your children to your friends from different professions. The earlier girls as well as boys understand their many career choices, the sooner they start to think about where their real interests lie.

- Encourage your children to talk with family friends and relatives who hold different jobs to find out what their responsibilities are, what education or training was required to get the position, what they like best or least about their job, etc.

- Explicitly comment on TV shows' and commercials' portrayal of females–and males–their messages about body image, relationships, sex, violence and incidences that demean someone's humanity.

- Educate your children–boys and girls–about sexual harassment. For younger kids, you may want to begin with a discussion of the difference between teasing and bullying, then move into a discussion about flirting vs. sexual harassment.

- Pay attention to the way you respond to "acting out" behavior. Note whether you treat or comment on girls and boys differently.

- There is a constructive way to approach gender bias. Both girls and boys have much to learn about how to halt the negative impact of sexism, and how to work cooperatively to accomplish this goal.

- Help your sons and daughters expect a future in which they are equally comfortable in their work and family roles.

Influencing school policies and practices

Given recent gender-focused educational research, what should parents look for in evaluating their current school or in considering an independent school for their children?

The decision to choose a single sex school depends on the needs and personality of your child. But in any event many of the characteristics of "successful" single sex classrooms are replicated in coed schools–a profound sense of responsibility for one's own learning and that of others; a spirit of cooperative-learning, with students feeling free to admit mistakes, ask questions, take risks and express confusion; and a warm rapport among teacher and students.

Experts suggest these policies and practices nurture girls' academic strengths; however, they are the building blocks for *all* academic success. Observe whether the teachers in your child's school include these practices in their classrooms. (You can tell only if you're there.) Encourage the integration of such reinforcing activities. Offer to help out in a classroom; have an "informational" (i.e., not crisis) conference with your child's teachers. When you're not focused on a specific problem and just "getting to know" a teacher, you can tell a lot about how he operates. Support a teacher's positive practices.

Schools need to foster an atmosphere and establish opportunities for true collaboration, such as a group project that no single child can complete without the group's help.

- Eliminate activities that pit boys against girls.

- Give girls as many opportunities to lead as boys are given.

- Acknowledge the accomplishments of women.

- Use alternative methods of teaching (especially in the math and science area) when a student doesn't understand a concept or process.

- Ensure that students' learning is assessed in many ways: tests, work samples taken at the beginning and ending of semesters, projects, self-assessment, teacher observation, etc.

- Encourage girls to act as experts, to choose leadership roles, and not be guided towards less demanding goals.

- Keep expectations high and give girls frequent feedback. Because girls often do not expect to do well in science and math, they tend to need more encouragement than boys.

- Give girls the opportunity to be in control of technology. In coed settings, consider an (after-school) all-girls computer club which may allow girls to develop more computer expertise.

- Connect mathematics, science, and technology to the real world, to the lives of real people and the good of the world.

- Be vigilant for gender bias, especially in interactions between children and classroom materials.

- Produce promotional materials that are gender-fair and devoid of stereotypes in written or pictorial images.

Examining your attitudes

Parents can begin by examining their own attitudes. Fathers deal with their own sense of masculinity, their own sense of being a man; mothers with being a woman and a mother.

Check your attitudes and casual comments:

- Do you allow boys to use poor grammar and profanity?
- Do you expect girls to be more dependent and/or less aggressive?
- Do you expect boys to be more aggressive and more independent?
- Do you disapprove of noisy girls more than noisy boys?
- Do you feel for girls who are unable or unwilling to be fashionable or call special attention to those who are fashionable?
- Do you feel for boys who are unable or unwilling to be athletic or call special attention to those who are athletic?
- Do you react negatively to boys who have long hair or girls with extremely short hair?
- Do you use slang terms such as sissy, fag, tomboy, chick, etc?
- Do you tend to discipline a daughter verbally and leniently, but a son physically and strictly?
- Do you expect girls to be more verbal and artistic than boys, or boys to be more mathematical and scientific than girls?

See also: Friendships, Harassment, Sexual Responsibility

RESOURCES

Center for Research on Women. Wellesley College. Wellesley, MA 02181 or call 617- 283-2500. Publishers of *How Schools Can Stop Shortchanging Girls (and Boys): Gender Equity Strategies.*

Girls Incorporated, 30 East 33rd Street, New York, NY 10016; 212-689-3700.

Ms. Foundation for Women, founders of Take Our Daughters To Work Day, 120 Wall Street, 33rd Floor, New York, NY 10005 or call 800-676-7780.

Failing at Fairness: How America's Schools Cheat Girls. Myra and David Sadker. New York: Charles Scribner's Sons.

Mother Daughter Revolution: From Betrayal to Power. Elizabeth Debold, Marie Wilson and Idelisse Malave. New York. Addison-Wesley Publishing Co.

School Girls: Young Women, Self Esteem, and the Confidence Gap. Peggy Orenstein/American Association of University Women, Doubleday.

The Courage to Raise Good Men. Olga Silverstein and Beth Rashbaum. New York: Penguin Books.

Harassment

"Boys will be boys." "She can't take a joke." "She asked for it by wearing those clothes." "It's just a part of school life. A lot of people do it. It's no big deal."

Remarks such as these supposedly justify subjecting adolescent girls to unwelcome sexually-tinged comments and suggestive physical acts during school and at social activities. Boys, too, are often the target of unwanted off-color remarks and suggestive touching by girls who justify their conduct as fun or flirtation. Boys who appear insufficiently macho may be routinely ridiculed as homosexual. Yet to the extent sexually harassing behaviors negatively affect a student's ability to benefit fully from educational opportunities and to enjoy a healthy school environment–as they most certainly do–they violate federal law.

There is little doubt that our children frequently encounter sexually harassing conduct in their schools, although many would not label it as such and are unaware that silent endurance is both unnecessary and self-defeating. Some conduct is blatant and would be recognized as harassment by anyone:

- A group of male athletes dresses up as cheerleaders for a school-sponsored skit, where they dance suggestively wearing signs saying "suck me" over their genitals.

- A class of fifth graders makes life miserable by teasing the one girl in the class who has mature breasts.
- Students gang up to pull down the pants of a boy or girl in the hallway.
- A girl "playfully" grabs and squeezes the genitals of a boy with whom she flirts.
- Boys comment on the "tits" and short skirts of their female classmates and circulate a list rating the physical attributes and sexual preferences of each.
- Boys decide one of their classmates is effeminate, and call him "faggot."

Other behaviors are slightly more subtle, but also offensive to those who are targeted:

- A school does nothing when girls complain about the showing of an explicit R-rated movie in class or at a school function.
- A boy continues to pursue a dating relationship with a girl who has repeatedly told him she is not interested, cornering her in the hallway and telephoning her each evening.
- Students wear sexually-suggestive T-shirts, or overly tight or brief clothing.
- Boys persistently laugh and snicker when girls speak up in class or ask questions, without reprimand from the teacher.
- Boys write sexual messages about various girls on bathroom and locker room walls.

None of these events is rare. In 1993, the American Association of University Women (AAUW) commissioned a survey of 1,632 students in grades 8 through 11 in 79 public schools around the U.S. That study concluded that four out of five students have experienced some sort of sexual harassment in school. A student's first experience with harassment is likely to occur in middle school. Eighty-five percent of the girls and 76 percent of the boys reported being the target of some form of unwanted sexual harassment that interfered with their lives. Thirty-one percent of the girls and 18 percent of the boys reported being targeted "often." Another study found no differences between public and private schools in the rates at which students report various forms of harassment.

Experts concur that sexual harassment, like rape and childhood abuse, is not primarily motivated by sexual feelings. It is an exercise of power and control, an attempt to make the recipient feel uncomfortable and inferior. Researcher Susan Strauss illustrates this point well by contrasting sexual harassment with appropriate flirting behavior:

Receiver of *harassment* feels:	**Receiver of *flirting* feels:**
Bad	Good
Angry/sad	Happy
Demeaned	Flattered
Ugly	Attractive
Powerless	In control

***Harassment* is perceived as:**	***Flirting* is perceived as:**
One-sided	Reciprocal
Demeaning	Flattering
Invading	Open
Degrading	Complimentary

***Harassment* results in:**	***Flirting* results in:**
Negative self-esteem	Positive self-esteem

***Harassment* is:**	***Flirting* is:**
Unwanted	Wanted
Power-motivated	Equality-motivated
Illegal	Legal

There is also little doubt that harassment at school and in related social situations is harmful to targeted students. First, it interferes with a young person's access to the education of her choice, and therefore seriously threatens her future occupation.

Nearly one in four of the students who reported harassment in the AAUW survey wanted to stay home from school or did so, and a similar percent reported not wanting to talk as much in class after experiencing harassment and/or reported that their grades were negatively affected. Second, harassment leads to psychological injury not unlike that suffered by victims of sexual assault. Sexual harassment victims feel afraid, have lowered self-esteem, experience more stress, have more frequent eating disorders and are at heightened risk of depression and suicide.

Give kids tools to avoid and confront

The first step parents can take to minimize exposure to sexual harassment is to see that the school has in place an explicit, well-disseminated policy outlawing sexually harassing behavior, together with clear procedures for students to report complaints, for sound investigation, and for the assigning of consistent consequences for violators. It is also helpful to urge the school to include instruction on sexual harassment issues and to sponsor mandatory consciousness-raising programs not only for students, but for staff as well. (The resources at the end of this chapter suggest curricula and procedures.)

Parents can also urge their children to object aggressively if faced with instances of harassing behavior, and support them when they do so. Experts believe that trying to ignore or go along with harassing behavior is to guarantee that it will continue; an assertive response is almost always more effective. As in many other areas, a child with a solid sense of self-worth is best armed to deal with demeaning comments and events, and to take appropriate action. Such a child is also able to say no persuasively or take no for an answer when dealing with members of the opposite sex.

Children should be cautioned against telling off-color stories in mixed company and warned not to comment on the sexual endowments/physical appearance or sexual preferences of their peers. Parents can discuss with their children what behavior is appropriate when an attraction is not reciprocated. To avoid giving offense in sexual and social matters is simply one more aspect of treating others with respect.

Children should be cautioned not to respond to an embarrassing situation by retaliating or finding a more vulnerable victim to harass. (In the AAUW survey, 17 percent of students reported that they had been called lesbian or gay when they didn't want to be, but of the boys who had suffered this particular form of abuse, more than half [58 percent] reported that they themselves had called someone else gay.)

Finally, we all recognize that our children model their behavior on what they see at home. In this area, as in many others, parents can lead by setting a good example. Laughing at a joke or a movie depicting a stereotypical bimbo or an abusive macho figure or commenting on the appearance or sexual orientation of others sends the wrong message to our youngsters.

*See also: Gender, Respect, Risky Business, School Rivalry,
Sexual Responsibilty*

RESOURCES

*Hostile Hallways: The AAUW Survey on Sexual Harassment in America's
Schools*, American Association of University Women Educational Foundation,
1993.

Secrets in Public: Sexual Harassment in Our Schools N. Stein, N. Marshall and
L. Tropp, , Wellesley College Center for Research on Women & NOW Legal
Defense and Education Fund, 1993.

Sexual Harassment and Teens: A Program for Positive Change, S. Strauss,
Free Spirit Publishing, Inc., 1993.

Media: Electronic Intelligence

Forget about religion and politics—the fiercest battles on the home-front these days probably concern electronic media—how much and what kinds of television to watch, which movies are okay, what CDs to buy, how much and what Internet access is acceptable. Between television, music, the Internet, video games, videotapes and films, today's children are plugged in as never before and exposed to influences, ideas and images that we as parents may find objectionable. And as children mature, it isn't simply a matter of turning off the set or not shelling out the bucks. It's a big world out there. Kids will hear lyrics and see programs that we probably won't like.

Like most parenting concerns, mental health experts agree that there is no substitute for well-informed parents who know their own children well. For instance, while music doesn't present much threat to the average teenager whose life is happy and healthy, a teenager who becomes preoccupied with music with seriously destructive themes and who seems to be growing more isolated and depressed or begins to abuse drugs or alcohol probably should be checked out by a mental health professional.

But what about the less extreme examples? How can parents begin to get a grip on an issue that has provoked so much national debate, emotional rhetoric and the V-chip? One organization that deals with the big-picture media issues is the Institute for Mental Health Initiatives (IMHI), a Washington-based group whose goal is to present the latest research in the behavioral sciences to the "creative community," meaning television and movie producers and music industry professionals. Its advisory board includes many mental health experts on children's issues as well as media representatives from groups such Fox Children's Network, MTV, MCA-Universal and the Children's Television Workshop.

One of the organization's initiatives focused on how portrayals of language, sex and violence can either pose risks to or help children between the ages of 7 and 13 as they grow into adolescence. Children in that age range, experts agree, are increasingly receptive (and therefore vulnerable) to influences outside their families. Teachers, coaches and other adults they meet as well as the characters they watch become increasingly important models of how to act, react and think.

The kids are paying close attention to how others manage to deal with emotions such as anger, frustration and sexuality. They are also still developing the capacity to manage their behavior and to consider the risks, goals and consequences of their actions. Consequently, media portrayals that suggest quick and easy answers to the tough work of building relationships, reigning in strong feelings and acting responsibly are often misleading and sometimes destructive. However, those that realistically depict how these issues play out for kids can provide terrific role models.

L(anguage)

Language is a hot-button issue as kids hit adolescence and learn to express themselves from the role models around them, whether they come from television, film, the school yard or their own homes. "If their models sound more like Howard Stern than Ted Koppel, so, too, might they," IMHI's report said. Kids are likely during this time to pick up on language to mock, bully or put others down. When they see no repudiation of such language, they may also accept the attitudes and beliefs about relationships that these forms of expression imply.

Children in this age group also are learning to substitute language for action, to listen, to joke and to communicate thoughts and feelings effectively. They will use language to define and assert who they are, and their choices and humor may not always please their parents. Shows like *Home Improvement* and *Seinfeld* are popular with children this age, IMHI's professionals point out, because of the way the characters interact. They share concerns and feelings; they listen and they temper their teasing with love. As they do, they demonstrate acceptance and the ability to express strong emotions without meanness–relationship skills 7-to-13-year-olds need to master.

S(ex) and V(iolence)

So what about the two big issues: sex and violence? Studies of young teenagers, according to IMHI, indicate a connection between watching sexually explicit shows and early initiation of sexual behavior. "Those that depict sexual conquest, and even rape, as the measure of manliness or seduction as a means of manipulation, may lead young viewers to see sex as a route to power rather than as an expression of love. Portrayals in which love and intimacy are absent, and especially where women are shown as the victims of sexual violence or disdain, can influence viewers' images of their own sexuality and of the opposite sex in negative ways."

Then there's the violence issue: research on the impact of viewing on-screen violence is consistent. Children who view lots of TV and film violence are more likely to become desensitized to real-world violence, to see the world as more violent than it is and to behave more aggressively themselves. Children are most likely to imitate violent behavior when it is effective, rewarded, has no consequences and is easy to copy. "Most on-screen violence is like this. It suggests that the fist or a weapon is mightier than the word and that nothing much bad happens when you use either. Children need to learn that this is not true," IMHI's professionals assert.

Challenging censorship

So is the answer more V-chips and censorship? "No," says Jon Katz, author of *Virtual Reality*. He recommends that censorship and bans should be the last resort in dealing with children, not the first. "Parents who thoughtlessly ban access to online culture or lyrics they don't like or understand, parents who exaggerate and distort the dangers from violent and pornographic imagery are acting out of their own anxiety and failing to prepare their children for the world they'll have to live in," he maintains.

In his "Cyberkid's Bill of Rights," Katz recommends, among other ideas, that children should have a right to explore for themselves what education, literacy and civic mindedness include. However, children's rights are not synonymous with permissiveness.

Experts agree that all children need clear boundaries and logical consequences for their behavior.

So what's the answer? Guide their choices, online and off. "As powerful as they are," says Katz, "media and culture or the sometimes offensive imagery transmitted by them can't form our children's value system or provide the building blocks of conscience. Only parents can do that. The idea that a TV show or lyric can transform a healthy, connected, grounded child into a dangerous monster is absurd. If we accompany them when they first turn on the TV or radio or set out online, showing them what is inappropriate and dangerous, we should have no need for external substitutes."

See also: Computers

Money: Developing Financial Responsibility

When Daniel got his driver's license at age 16, his parents were relieved to buy him a car so he could drive himself to school from their distant suburban neighborhood. The new Volvo cost more than $35,000. Cars driven by students attending local schools are sometimes newer and worth considerably more than those driven by the faculty. It's a significant symbol of the affluence–and, some say, the parental indulgence– of our area.

In another family, when the teen commented on how great it would be to have her own car–preferably a red convertible–the parents asked her if she would like to own a car or continue attending the independent school she loved. Put that way, in terms of affordability and priorities, the car was a distant second choice.

How can our children, who have friends carrying wallets stuffed with credit cards and cash, learn the value of money when they are exposed to such affluence and when we give them so much, so often, so readily?

One way is by talking to our children about money from an early age, as the seemingly endless questions come up on the subject so that children learn both values and the value of money bit by bit. Be open with your kids; discuss their questions with them as they come up instead of putting them off. Let your children hear you and your spouse discuss some family finances. That way they learn about the family income and budget in a context.

Allowances

Delayed gratification and learning to evaluate whether a purchase is really worth the expense are just a few of the lessons learned when kids get allowances and start to manage their own money, financial managers and parent educators agree. Allowances teach children management skills at a young age, a skill that is especially critical during the first few years away from home when so many young people find themselves in credit card disaster.

Parents should keep allowance systems simple and easy to administer. Certain expenses should become the responsibility of the child, such as charitable contributions, video games, movies, or other agreed upon items. As we expand their allowance, we can expand their responsibilities with it, so that by the time they are in high school they may be able to manage their own clothing budget.

At the Parent Encouragement Program (PEP), a family education center in Kensington, parent educators advise families to base allowances on a child's age and interests, needs and wants, individual family's resources, and parents' beliefs. PEP advocates that once allowances are given and training in money management has been provided, control should be turned over to allow the child to learn from his own mistakes.

"That's where it gets hard," said Linda Jessup, director of PEP. "Many parents have trouble with this, because they don't want to see their child waste his money, but mistakes are where so much of the child's real learning takes place."

Allowances can train children to start budgeting for their own kinds of expenses, as well as to provide the opportunity for learning what it means to donate for religious or charitable purposes from their own cash and conscience, not just the family's budget. "Some to live, some to give, and some to save" are the three basic considerations for planning an allowance, suggests Jessup.

Allowances require discipline on the parents' part as well, the commitment to pay on the day agreed upon. No excuses, the experts say. If you make an agreement about an amount, you must pay up as promised.

Chores

Should children be required to do chores in exchange for allowances? Again that is a decision families make based on their own finances and personal values. One school of thought says that children should learn that money is what you get for hard work well done. Chores done well and on time are rewarded with pay (allowances) and that teaches the way of the working world. But others cite surveys that show that parents lose track of whether chores have been performed–something kids count on–and parents often end up paying their children allowances anyway.

Still others argue that children paid for chores stop doing those jobs once they can earn better wages outside the home. Worse, they say, is that a valuable teaching opportunity has been missed, that people who share household chores do so because they live there and care about one another. Many families view an allowance as their child's share of the family resources–not to be withheld. And chores can be considered the child's portion of family responsibility–something not to be left undone.

Jobs

Most financial educators agree that children should have opportunities to earn extra cash beyond allowances by doing extra jobs around the house, yard and neighborhood. Not only does that teach delayed gratification, an essential element in money management, by providing savings opportunities, but it also adds to the child's education about the real cost of status labels and whether they are worth it to purchase. "I tell my daughter my job is to buy her jeans, but if she wants the designer label, the extra cost has to come out of her budget, not mine," says a Potomac lawyer and mother of a 14-year-old.

Area parents report that children who work extra or save longer for the designer labels have learned valuable lessons: their kids either start taking better care of their expensive clothes because they worked so hard to obtain them, or they decide they are less enthusiastic about status labels because they find they are not worth the extra saving or sweat equity in the long run.

"You would be amazed how many times my daughter decides not to buy something because she has to use her own money, or how many times we have returned something because the quality just wasn't good enough at that price, when she bought it with her own money," said the mother of a 13-year-old.

While a job may increase a teen's level of responsibility, researchers at Temple University recently concluded that teenagers who work more than 15 hours weekly have a decreased interest in school that translates into poorer grades and a shrinking interest in their education. They also found that working long hours was associated with increasing "antisocial activity," school misconduct, and drug and alcohol use.

How to use money earned during the summer should be discussed before the job begins. In many families these earnings are designated as bankable discretionary college funds. Some families find that the additional stress of balancing an after-school job frequently outweighs any life learning or earning that comes with such a responsibility. Parents can feel comfortable telling their high-schooler, "Your job right now is school."

Matching funds

Some parents have a hard time seeing their children do without material things the parents might have missed in their own childhood, so they shower those items on their children. A mistake, the experts agree, that breeds "ungrateful kids" who develop a sense of entitlement and without a sense of responsibility. A reverse mistake, the experts say, is when parents require their children to work for every dollar in order to develop what they would call a realistic money sense, resulting in children with poverty mentality. To avoid that, some experts suggest that parents provide a matching fund for earnings and/or savings put towards a coveted item. For example, if a child achieves the goal of working and saving toward a new tennis racket, the parent will provide matching funds for lessons or new shoes.

Credit cards

In dual-career areas such as metropolitan Washington, where incomes tend to be higher and family time limited, it is not uncommon to see parents giving children their credit cards for clothing and other purchases. Parents do this as a sign of trust. Some financial experts suggest that limited, controlled teenage use of credit cards can be positive, but giving kids unlimited use of the parents' credit card or giving kids their own brings out just the qualities that should be avoided. Kids can begin to feel that their money supply will always be there. To avoid this development, experts say parents should consider giving a credit card for a specific purchase, but setting a limit the parent would be willing to cover for that purpose.

Often parents reserve the use of credit cards until their students are in college, where they can be designated (*in advance*) for emergency use or for travel expenses. Many parents choose not to give their kids credit cards but instead help them learn to budget with bank books, personal finance notebooks and money-review sessions. Showing children the credit card bills and having them watch as parents write a check for each bill helps kids see the important connection between plastic and real money.

Developing fiscal responsibilities

Money managers and parent educators offer the following tips and strategies for teaching children how to assume fiscal responsibilities:

- *Try a subscription to the magazine Zillions,* a well-written Consumer Union publication for kids that aims to teach them how to be savvy consumers.

- *Consider giving allowances on Monday* instead of weekends, which often builds in a buffer zone for delayed gratification before the lures of weekend spending.

- *Have your child keep track of his spending* for a few weeks before his allowance amount is set to help decide how much to give. Review allowance amounts at least annually, perhaps at the beginning of each school year. It's a great time to monitor expenditures.

- *Practice not lending a child money for a spontaneous purchase* of items seen while at the mall. Some experts consider this the beginning of a credit-spending habit. Rather, delay the purchase until the next trip to the mall. This gives the child time to review and perhaps rethink her decision, delay the gratification of purchase, and buy with cash, not credit.

- *Consider dividing allowances into three jars,* one for living, one for savings and one for charity or giving. This gives kids a visual image to help develop their money management skills.

- *Deposit savings into a bank account in the child's name* at regular intervals, insisting on a passbook, so the child can see each transaction grow.

- *Post a list of optional jobs for pay on the family bulletin board* or other prominent spot and include the date or time of day by which the work must be completed and at what price. Remind kids that you pay only for jobs done reasonably well, not for sloppy work.

• Consider drawing your older child into the world of investments by buying some shares of stock in a child friendly company (McDonald's, Disney) or a local business (Giant). Teach the child what you know about the stock market, how to track company earnings, and if you don't know yourself, find a way for you and your child to learn together. (There are some good books on "the market" for beginners.)

• Remember that parents provide the strongest model for their children about money management for fun and profit and as a tool for living. Many family financial advisors report that the best thing parents can do is to set limits on their child's access to money. This encourages a child to become a decision maker, to make choices, so that he will not become the "passive spender" he can so easily turn into when money is open-ended.

See also: Driving, Shoplifting, Shopping Malls, Yes!

No! And Meaning It

"Joey doesn't have a curfew," one boy explained, "because his parents don't care."

Setting limits and sticking to them is seldom easy. Many parents have a hard time saying "no"–and an even harder time following through. "Parents, like schools, have to decide on the most important issues on which to "draw the line." With adolescents, there are many issues that provide opportunities to teach decision making and its consequences," says Headmistress Agnes Underwood.

"Kids feel safer when they are given clear limits," notes Dr. Sally L. Smith, nationally recognized educator. "Even if they revolt against them, they feel better knowing that there are parameters and boundaries." Helping our children behave in an acceptable manner is a necessary part of raising our children well. Changing our children's unwanted behaviors–or preventing potentially undesirable ones–helps them develop the self-control they need to become responsible and considerate of others.

"Parental guidance translates into love," says Joanne Ricciardiello, president of PANDAA (Parents' Association to Neutralize Drug and Alcohol Abuse). "Children appreciate limits." When we set limits, we must be prepared to define "why." There will be times when it will be necessary to say, "No, because I am the parent," or as one quick-thinking mother replied in answer to her teenage son, "Because that's my job." With parents guiding the process by setting consistent, reasonable limits, self-control increases throughout the school years. Teenage experimentation and rebellion may occur, but the vast majority of adolescents pass through this period to become responsible adults.

Why set limits?

As parents today, we have to be vigilant because of the many dangerous opportunities available to our children. Peer pressure is intense, and participation in risky behavior is often perceived as evidence of being "cool." We must not be so concerned about our children's popularity and losing their love that we condone questionable behavior. Parents who worry that they will lose their children's love should heed Brown University psychologist Brian Hayden's counsel: "Parents who set no limits wind up rejected by teenagers who may never learn how to create their own limits. Rejection is also the likely fate of parents who opt to become their teens' all-understanding friend."

Overindulged children are "immediate gratification" children who don't set goals, don't have tenacity for life, and feel outraged and mistreated if they don't get what they want. They have a high suicide rate and are at high risk for recreational drug and alcohol use and promiscuous sex, according to Linda Jessup, founder and director of PEP. She also cautions us that children of highly authoritarian parents are at greater risk of getting involved in violent crime, using hard drugs, and becoming alcoholics. "Children who learn from an early age that they must experience the consequences of their choices and actions will grow into thoughtful adults with the confidence and ability to solve their own problems," she advises. Children whose parents are fair and use consequences rather than punishment will learn to "draw the line" for themselves.

The way we correct our child or adolescent for misbehavior should suit the misconduct and make sense. The consequences should not be so strict that the child can't later feel the parent's love and good intentions. For example, we don't need to ground a child for a month if he misses curfew by 15 minutes one evening. Similarly, it makes no sense to deny telephone privileges for an extended period for a minor infraction. Children of overly strict parents are at just as much risk for dangerous behaviors as are children of indulgent parents. Emphasizing control instead of learning about the consequences of an action prevents a child from gaining the experience needed to become a responsible adult who can make informed decisions.

Drawing the line

We must remember that it is our *right* and *responsibility* as a parent to say "no." Adolescents are no longer children, but neither are they adults, yet. There are certain situations where "no" is not negotiable. We must say "no":

- *To activities that seriously interfere with academic success,* such as part-time jobs, overly demanding hobbies and social outings.

- *To destructive relationships.* This must be done very carefully, perhaps with the help of a professional counselor, so as not to drive our child further into the relationship.

- *To drugs and underage drinking.* Remember that the legal drinking age in all area jurisdictions is 21, so that *all* drinking by high school students and younger, regardless of where it takes place, is illegal.

- *To any activity which seems questionable,* regardless of how much our child protests, and regardless of what "everyone else is doing." Says psychologist Hayden, "The world is a fragmented social milieu of MTV, AIDS, drugs, sex and too many choices for children who are in no way developmentally ready to make these choices. 'No' is an anchor...."

- *To compromising our values,* no matter how much they are resisted, and no matter what others say or do. Resistance is normal. Never forget how important we and our value system are to a child or adolescent experiencing confusing changes and intense emotions. When we impart our values to our children, we reinforce our commitment and caring.

A positive approach

There are also some important "positives" to keep in mind when setting limits. Limit-setting, discipline, and consequences are not punishment; they are ways of teaching acceptable behavior that enables our children to function productively in society. Limit-setting is a way of imparting our values. Early adolescence is a time when our teens are struggling to define personal values and direction. For some teens, points out Hayden, "The dependency on home and parents is summarily abandoned for what is called 'freedom' but what is instead a kind of slavery to the dictates of the peer group."

"Clearly establishing a line ahead of time, and steadfastly acknowledging that line after the fact, together serve to make the...policy unambiguous and fair," according to Headmaster Damon Bradley. "I can think of no worse lesson than emphasizing a position ahead of time, and then negotiating it away after an incident. Drawing a line suggests a boundary not to be crossed."

Defining values in terms of clear limits should start early–very early. In other words, we can't wait until puberty–when our child might be bigger than we, mobile, and capable of resistance–to begin to teach values, spend time together, and set and enforce limits. Keeping unwanted behavior from happening in the first place is easier than stopping it later.

Fairness, good listening skills, consistency, and what sometimes seems like a superhuman fund of patience are critical tools for successful limit-setting. A healthy sense of humor and perspective also are invaluable. "The issue," said Headmaster Dr. Elliot Prager, "is not [which] movie is appropriate for a 13-year-old; no doubt we will disagree...on definitions of 'appropriate.' The issue is, however, establishing limits for our children, clarifying for them what the family's values are, and drawing the line beyond which we are prepared to say, 'This is not acceptable.'"

Components of successful limit-setting

- *Regularly reinforcing and positively encouraging our children.* It's easier for our children to avoid doing wrong when they're consistently supported for what they're doing right.

- *Establishing and communicating the family's rules and values.*

- *Providing for a reasonable amount of family time together.* Some relaxed time focused on the family is necessary for healthy emotional development. It also gives parents and children a sound basis for building mutual respect and keeping the lines of communication open.

- *Agreeing upon clear behavioral expectations.*

- *Writing down the rules, if necessary, along with the consequences* for breaking them, and giving our children a copy–and/or posting them someplace visible. (Many youngsters, particularly those with learning differences, have difficulty processing information auditorily.)

- *Making the "punishment" fit the crime.* Consequences should suit the misconduct and make sense.

- *Discussing consequences with our children ahead of time,* remembering that parents need to have the final say. If given the opportunity, youngsters often will come up with surprisingly suitable consequences for breaking the rules.

- *Supporting our child if they get caught* cheating/shoplifting/ drinking, without excusing the behavior. Psychologists recommend that our child not only receive the "legally" assigned punishment, but also an additional consequence designed and agreed upon by both parents and child.

- *Negotiating limits with our children regularly and individually.* Remember that for adolescents especially, this is an age of many firsts: a first date, a driver's license, the first awareness of emerging sexuality, the first prom, the first evenings out of the house alone–all occasions for solidifying appropriate expectations.

- *Being willing to admit our mistakes,* acknowledging that sometimes we are wrong. Parents occasionally set limits that turn out to be unreasonable, unrealistic or inappropriate. We need to also model change and a willingness to negotiate. By being flexible, we are doing our teens a genuine service.

- *Allowing our children to be different within limits,* to pick our battles thoughtfully. We can expect our child to adopt different dress, language and behaviors as part of the separation process within reasonable limits. If we're unsure about what constitutes reasonable limits, we can talk with other parents who share our values, and consult with the school. Consistently inappropriate behavior, lying, rule breaking, school problems, moodiness or withdrawal, and excessive time away from home may be signs of more serious problems that should be addressed immediately and professionally.

- *Getting to know the parents of our children's classmates.* This will alert us to any potential problems over differences in parenting styles. It's also easier to enforce limits consistently when we know others who are experiencing similar challenges with their children.

- *Consistently checking arrangements with parents of our child's friends,* regardless of what she tells you. Adolescents occasionally try to "pull a fast one" by saying they are going to a friend's house and then going somewhere else. If our children object to our "checking up" on them, explain that it's not a matter of trust, just verification that the other parents are in agreement with their plans.

- *Eliminating unnecessary rules,* so the ones we have will be remembered—advice frequently given to parents of preschool children.

- *Following up immediately when trouble is suspected.*

When we "draw the line" and follow through, we are modeling just what we want our children to be able to do—when faced with temptations, to internalize their own limits. If we can make thoughtful decisions, consider the consequences, and avoid compromising their values, they can become adults who can confidently do "the right thing."

See also: Communicating, Risky Business, Yes!

Parties

The prospect of hosting or having their children attending parties always gives parents pause. As children grow older, factoring the "fun" quotient quickly becomes overshadowed by the concern for finding safe, age-appropriate activities. Teenagers, who should and usually do have a hand in planning their own parties, are not always able to identify potentially dangerous situations, and are sometimes overwhelmed by peer pressure into doing things they know they shouldn't.

Providing a healthy social climate for your child tests key parental duties: setting limits, conveying values and fostering responsibility. All these involve discussion and joint problem-solving with your children. The general rule of thumb for all parents is to make it as hard as possible for your kids to get in trouble, no matter the age.

Parties can be a major pitfall. Some parents have a hard time setting limits and sticking to them, so each year raucous behavior and police intervention happen as a result of gatherings that get out of hand or chaperones who fail in their roles.

Some parents are caught up in whether their child is a social butterfly; they feel embarrassed if their child is not in the "popular" group, or doesn't get invited to the homecoming dance or prom. Often parents equate their children's social success with being in a particular group. Unfortunately, that group may be the one that is drinking, doing drugs, smoking, and going to inappropriate parties.

Even social events for grade schoolers can go awry through a lack of clear guidelines or insensitive strategies about who and how many to invite.

Grade schoolers

Parties that are built around specific activities work best. Children at this age should be involved in basic party planning. They can help with the decisions on the kind of party, the friends they want to be sure to include and the appearance of the invitations. (Computer-generated "originals" can be fun and easy for a child to produce.) A widely followed guideline for invitations is to invite a number less than half the class, or the whole class. Invitations should be made by mail if possible, so details are available and clear and so children who are not included will not be hurt. A handy guest list ensures that parents who RSVP can more easily organize carpools. Let your children know how you expect them to behave. Then *be there* from beginning to end.

Middle schoolers

The issue of boy-girl parties first arises as problematic in this age range. Different rates of maturation call for these events to have small guest lists and, once again, well-defined activities. It's more important than ever for parents to discuss the nature of the party, chaperone rules and definite hours with their child. Parents should know which children will be invited, and should make it clear that a chaperone will always be on hand, whether he sits behind a group of kids at a movie theater or nearby at a pool party, or is just in and out of the room on a frequent basis.

High schoolers

It is difficult and sometimes impossible to control all factors of teenage parties, so it is most important for parents and teens to come up with a party plan and set limits. If your teen is hosting a party, make sure you are home for its entire run and that you actually circulate among the guests from time to time. In general, it is advisable to have one adult chaperone for every 10 guests; for parties of more than 20, there should be an additional chaperone for every five to 10 extra guests.

Limit attendance. Drinking should not be allowed; if a guest arrives drunk, make the necessary arrangements but do not let that guest stay. Let your neighbors know about the party, particularly if parking or outside noise is a consideration.

The rules agreed to in advance should be specific. These might include: no drinking, no smoking; no leaving the party and then returning; lights left on; some rooms in the house off-limits. Discuss how to handle unexpected situations.

Parent networking

If your teen is going to a party, parent networking beforehand is even more important. Communicate with the host's parents and find out what the party rules are. Make sure there will be chaperones on hand. Establish a curfew for your child, and work on refusal skills when he is faced with the offer of a drink.

Most open parties happen when parents are out of town and have left a teen home alone. A few invited friends can end up facing hundreds of gate crashers who can damage property or provide drugs and alcohol. Parents who fail to supervise their teenager's party and/ or allow illegal substances on their property may be held criminally and civilly liable if someone, including the minor who consumed the substance, is injured as a result of the youngster's intoxication. This can result in a judgment against the homeowner.

An increasing number of community coalitions offer advice on party strategies, and even publish monthly lists of teen parties that warranted police attention–addresses included. Some PTAs ask parents to sign pledges, promising if they host a party it will be an adult-supervised gathering that will be alcohol- and drug-free, and publish a list of parents who have so pledged in the school newsletter.

A special note about sleepovers: Inviting small numbers of all-boys or all-girls works for younger ages. But coed events, usually held after the prom or graduation, can easily get out of hand. After-prom parties for all seniors can work best if space for dozing is well defined and adequately chaperoned with enough carpeted floor areas and comfortable furniture. Or buck the current trend and politely decline to host or allow your children to attend coed sleep-overs. If we work *with* our children, they can be happy, confident party-goers and we can be comfortable with their social activities.

See also: Alcohol, Communicating, Dating, Risky Business, Sexual Responsibility, Smoking

The Push For Success

An 18-year-old first-round draft pick of the Mets in 1995–a California kid who baseball scouts agreed had the hands, speed, and discipline to justify his $850,000 signing bonus and become a major league short-stop–quit baseball less than a year later, declaring in his four-page resignation letter that he really did not like the game and that his father had pushed him into it.

"This was bothering me and haunting me every day," the young man told the New York Times. *"I needed to move on and be happy. I've always pleased others instead of being happy for myself."*

Whether "success" is spelled by the number of zeroes in a signing bonus or, frequently in our well-educated, ambition-driven capitol region, based on the degrees after a person's name (the more ivy-league the better), parents need to appreciate that "success" that is parent-driven, not child-propelled, often comes at a great price.

"If only parents could see the suffering I see in kids all the time in my work, the depression caused by these parents who are pushing their kids on to 'success,'" commented educational psychologist William Stixrud. He acknowledges that parents who consider school acceptance the pinnacle of "success" often pressure their children because they love them and want them to experience the widest life choices available. However, the academic pressure parents apply from first grade forward increases the likelihood of burnout, physical ailments, depression, eating disorders and alienation. The push for success is fueled by parents suffering from the misguided notion that if children don't do well from the earliest years through high school, they won't be accepted into a good college, and later a good job, and ultimately will miss out on "the good life." As parents, we need to examine what we mean by "the good life." Is this our children's definition?

Choosing college

Bethesda career counselor Kaye Cook, who works with adolescents and adults, couldn't agree more. There is the temptation, she observes, to get kids into college right after high school because they don't have any other responsibilities then, "…but the truth is that some kids are just not ready for college at 17 or 18, and need more time to think through what they really want, and maybe shouldn't go to college at all."

And many parents do fear that if children take time off before college, they may not ever attend and complete a college program. "I can't relax and feel that my job is over until my child has at least a baseline college education," one mother said.

But there are a few young people who benefit from college only when they see a reason for it and (perhaps) pay for it themselves, and there are some who would profit from taking some well-planned time off from school before beginning a college program. "Not in a hedonistic sense, but in the realistic sense that work life will be long and stretched out. Life expectations will reach into the 80s and 90s for the next generation, so there is time to take, as long as they do this with a plan," Cook advises.

U.S. Department of Labor statistics show that the next generation is expected to experience seven to ten changes in jobs and four to five different careers during their working life, requiring ongoing training, recertification, and advanced degrees. Cook points out, "With kids realizing they probably won't be at a company long enough to collect a pension, since people change jobs every 3.6 years in this country, and Social Security won't take effect until a later age, the idea of education, then work, then a leisurely retirement with travel is an old idea that probably won't be there for this generation."

Before attending college some students consider established opportunities such as the Peace Corps or AmeriCorps or perhaps one of the more structured corporate or community service intern programs. These activities can give high school graduates a "window" on fields they are considering or provide new opportunities in addition to fostering more insight about themselves. Life experiences broaden our outlook at any age. The young person who serves in the Israeli army or as a nanny in Australia may be better prepared afterward to commit to the rigors of higher education.

It's her/his life

Parents can advise their children to acquire life skills through summer jobs, after-school jobs, internships, and community service projects, and on the importance of networking early with former teachers. High school graduates, even those who know what they want to do, can conduct informational interviews with people who have become successful in the fields they are considering and spend some days "shadowing" them to see what typical days on the job are really like. Teens can ask them who is the ideal person for the job, where the field is going, and then ask themselves if that is where they want to be going, too.

Parents should play a major role in this planning process, Cook advises, and not resist their child's ideas and desires, especially if they don't match the parents' hopes or expectations. The process of allowing your child to "control his destiny" is especially difficult when the child's intellectual curiosity, personal style or competitive spirit is not the same as the parents'. "Kids sing their song from the minute they are born, and parents need to be sensitive to their children's strengths and interests and explore with them what is out there, and not decide for them which way is best for them to go," Cook said.

What are their interests, their passions? Parents should be willing to take the time to ask the right questions and be astute observers of their children. What motivates them? Kids who make their own choices about what they want to do will be motivated to do what it takes to succeed.

And how can parents contribute to the success of the child who is ready for college? By taking a very active role in helping kids acquire all the information and choices for college, whether two-year, four-year, technical, or vocational. By making sure they have access to all the aptitude and assessment tests available. Parents can say "You may choose not to act on any of this information about college or career choices or vocations, but not knowing about it all is not an option. You must at least inform yourself."

Help your children focus on their gifts, interests and values throughout all their school years. Help them explore options that interest them and then help them find a college that provides an environment and curriculum to nourish these attributes. Parents and their children can research and experience the college cultures very carefully to make sure there is a "match" between those attributes and the strengths of the school. Listen to your children. And, perhaps most importantly, help your children trust their instincts when choosing this next step in life. Support their decisions.

Children need to be encouraged as they learn to make the choices in their lives, and be allowed to experience the positive and negative outcomes of their actions. As they do, they become better acquainted with their own needs and are more likely to find not only the path that is right for them but also the confidence to follow it.

See also: Depression, Eating, Sports, Stress

Respect for Diversity: Race, Religion, Culture…

When many of us were students, well-intentioned progressive teachers sought to instill in us the virtues of tolerance and color blindness. We were to "tolerate" those different from ourselves and to pretend the differences did not exist. A memorable ditty of that more innocent era went, "As the peach pit said to the apple core, the color of our skin doesn't matter any more." Well, it does matter. Today we know that these views are far too limited for a society whose goals are that all groups feel valued, at ease and comfortable with their differences.

Our region provides ample opportunity for friendships among diverse children. The nation's largest black upper-middle and middle classes have been a vital part of our area for over 100 years. The international population is vast, including immigrants, diplomats, and many other foreign professionals. The religious and economic mixture is no less varied. And of course, as the nation's capital, we attract Americans from every state, further enriching the mix of cultures and backgrounds.

Within the family

As parents, we can encourage our children's involvement with those different from ourselves and offer guidance in addressing all peers with respect. We can be prepared to address the issue of racial, religious or cultural bigotry whenever and wherever the opportunity arises. Parental techniques designed to achieve a balanced perspective include:

Modeling appropriate behavior. This includes zero tolerance for racial, religious or cultural epithets, and showing respect for and openness to other cultures through both our language and our behavior. Often children learn offensive responses from their most familiar environments—school, peers and family.

Respecting a child's reality. It is counterproductive to pretend that racial, religious and cultural differences do not exist. A child may describe a peer as "black," "brown," "Asian" or "Jewish." These attributes are too obvious to ignore, nor do we need to teach that ignoring them is necessary. But we can encourage our child to share details with us about a classmate who is described as "different." We can learn about Jewish/Christian/Islamic religious differences in an open way that encourages our child to appreciate the perspective of others. We can respect the beliefs of others as worthwhile while maintaining our own faith, and seek to relate respect and love for others to our own religious and cultural traditions.

Encouraging diverse friendships. A child should not be "told" to try to make friends different from herself, but we can encourage our children's friendships with children from different backgrounds. When invitations to birthday parties are doled out, ask, "Is my child including/excluding a group of classmates? Have I made friends with parents from other ethnic groups? Do *I* have a diverse group of social friends?" What we do speaks louder than all of our words.

Discouraging stereotype formation. This is perhaps the toughest task, as stereotypes often form from the kernel of a truth. For instance, many schools have made a conscious effort to diversify their student bodies by providing financial aid to select students. However, plenty of middle class and affluent minority children attend private schools; it is offensive to assume they are "affirmative action admissions." We should intervene firmly when our child or his peers engage in any stereotyping by immediately challenging such remarks, pointing out what is not only hurtful but also inaccurate. It is vital to clarify our own thinking before correcting our children.

Commenting on media images. We can teach our children to watch TV and movies with a critical eye. Minorities are often portrayed as one-dimensional criminals or terrorists or objects of fear, humor, or ridicule. We need to discuss the portrayal of people from different racial, cultural and religious groups and the messages about relationships, violence, humor, and jobs associated with different peoples. We may be trying to overcome a negative image, such as portrayal of people of certain groups as uniformly violent or unsavory, or we can note positive images ("Isn't she clever/sensitive/smart?" or "Now that's a great dad"). Parents can also point out similarities as well as differences between people. We may identify with a character who is clumsy, distractable, or generous whether or not his background is the same as ours. Traditional family celebrations are often enjoyable ways to share our culture and learn about others'.

Refusing to laugh at or tell biased jokes. Telling jokes is one of the most insidious ways in which people are harassed. We can influence our children by never telling biased jokes or making innuendoes and by openly objecting when others do. Point out that jokes based on stereotyped ethnic, racial or other characteristics ought to be insulting to all people—not just those who belong to the group being maligned. Polish, redneck and blonde jokes are not universally laughing matters.

Seeking out cross-cultural experiences. In our area there are many events, parades, concerts, picnics, fairs and sports, that attract a multiracial and multigenerational audience which we can attend together as a family or recommend to our teenager. We can encourage our children to invite a friend to attend a Greek festival in the suburbs or a Vietnamese market in Virginia or accept a friend's invitation to a Passover seder or other religious celebration in a tradition different from our own. Participation in one of the many international festivals at local schools or communities celebrating the diversity of their populations helps our children celebrate the diversity of our population.

Lastly, we have to be prepared for situations in which our child may be a victim of racial, religious, cultural or other types of intolerance or gender or sexual harassment, or may be concerned about a friend who is being victimized. What can we do? How should we react? One response is the "five step program." Although created for younger kids, the steps work just as well for preteen and teens (and adults!):

1. Ignore,

2. Respond in a friendly manner,

3. Respond in a firm manner,

4. Go away, and

5. Get an adult to help!

By the time such a problem is brought to our attention, it may very well be at the last stage–where adult intervention is required to protect the dignity of the child. It is important to keep in mind that children sometimes have volatile friendships and that name calling can be a fad or a game. Nonetheless, we do have to convey to our children that labeling someone with a negative racial, religious or cultural slur is not appropriate and will not be tolerated, even as part of an otherwise ordinary classroom disagreement. Most schools have explicit policies and behavior codes against malicious name calling and it is important to require students to live up to them. In extreme cases, legal prohibitions against racial, religious, sexual orientation and ethnic harassment may result in serious consequences for violators.

We needn't assume that misbehavior or an expression of narrow-minded opinion by a student necessarily originates in that child's home. Sometimes in the quest to establish a strong identity, a child will, in an effort to boost his own self-esteem, express dislike of those who are "different." We've all heard of the exclusive cliques and gangs that can plague school administrators. A lack of self-esteem can be transformed into disrespect (in extreme cases even hatred) for others. Children are naturally competitive, as are adults, but the feelings of others should be considered.

At school

Some educators think that, ideally, each child should have the experience of being in both the minority and in the majority at some point in her school career in order to gain appreciation of both per-spectives and to learn to live in a diverse society. While it is rarely feasible to change schools with this goal in mind, some local inde-pendent schools have introduced programs to foster better under-standing of what it's like to be different. Kids are encouraged to think about "walking in someone else's shoes" and trying to imagine what it might be like to be in a "minority" position in their school–if they are not.

Some area schools have introduced "Diversity Day" programs designed to increase sensitivity and empathy towards others. In one school, each 8th grade student is designated an outcast for one day. Students are shunned for wearing a blue shirt, having a June birth-day or for some other innocuous reason. They learn firsthand how it feels to be ignored or made to do meaningless tasks. Other schools have multicultural organizations, diversity conferences, student discussions on race, and courses on race, ethnicity and gender. Some teachers attend courses on diversity, such as those offered by the Black Student Fund, to better understand and support the development of all children in their classes.

Identities

Our children are forming their identities. An identity consists of many components, one of which is undoubtedly ethnic, racial or religious. This is healthy growth essential to the blossoming of a young adult. It is no coincidence that traditional rituals of initiation to religious or cultural traditions are held when the child is old enough to understand the concept of such identities, first communion, bar or bat mitzvah and debutante cotillions, to name a few. To be respectful of the traditions of others, our children need to feel secure in their own culture.

Valuing diversity benefits everyone. It does a child no good to think that he is better than someone else simply because society has privileged his ethnic, religious or social group. It is up to us to see that our children's maturing sense of identity includes not only strong identification with our own traditions, but also respect for and celebration of qualities people of divergent cultures have to offer.

See also: Friendships, Gender, Harassment, School Rivalry, Sports, Vandalism

RESOURCES

Different and Wonderful: Raising Black Children in a Race-Conscious Society. Drs. Darlene Powell Hopson and Derek S. Hopson. New York, NY: Simon & Schuster. 1992.

40 Ways to Raise a Nonracist Child. Barbara Mathias and Mary Ann French. New York, NY: Harper Collins. 1997.

Raising the Rainbow Generation: Teaching Your Children to be Successful in a Multicultural Society. Drs. Darlene Powell Hopson and Derek S. Hopson. New York: Simon & Schuster. 1993.

Respecting Our Differences: A Guide to Getting Along in a Changing World. Lynn Duvall. 1994.

Risky Business: Thrill Seeking

"She told me she was going to a movie. When I came to pick her up, she was getting out of someone's car. Her friends talked her into going to a bar."

"You must be mistaken; my son is in bed," the parent told the midnight caller. "No," came the reply, "he's standing in my foyer and I have a front yard covered with toilet tissue!"

"I opened a drawer one day and found it crammed full of lipsticks. Under pressure, my daughter admitted that she and her friends had been shoplifting."

"My son was out with a couple of friends. He saw the driver drink several beers—and still got into the car with him and rode around the beltway."

Our teens sometimes overstep boundaries, throw caution and good judgment to the wind, and indulge in risky behavior. Any "good" teenager, who would never initiate risky behavior, can be vulnerable to the contagion of peers who do. Some teenagers take risks, but because they have had strong guidance from parents, will know when to stop. Then there are a very few truly misguided kids who pursue risks for identity, attention or just plain "thrills."

"Adolescent behavior is unpredictable," counsels Robin Goldstein, Maryland child development specialist and author. "They are separating from their parents, and trying to establish their own identity and value system. As our teens experiment with independence and emerge into adulthood, they oscillate between behavior that shows good judgment and behavior that shows poor judgment, by taking risks and making decisions which are not sound."

Our teens can "experiment with independence," face peer pressure and be rebellious without risking their lives. Adolescent specialists caution that children who seek the "high" of courting danger or the perverse excitement of not getting caught for doing something wrong, often feel ignored or neglected by their parents. Thrill-seeking can be a sign of a serious problem; whether our child is the initiator or the follower in these kinds of behavior, we should not dismiss them as teenage "pranks."

Tackling challenges like rock climbing, platform diving, running for school office, performing in a play or competing in sports promotes self-confidence, personal growth, and maturity in young adults. Taking these kinds of risks stimulates growth and defines character. These are the types of activities we should encourage our children to do.

Resisting temptations

As parents we can help our teens develop skills to resist temptations such as reckless driving, drinking, sex, shoplifting and throwing parties in unsupervised homes. Our children need strong guidance to become more responsible, to be able to resist involvement in risky behaviors, to learn about peer pressure, to stay safe. If our child values our relationship, it will help her to follow the rules you feel strongly about. Respect is fostered by understanding, non-threatening communication and mutual adherence to rules. Goldstein reminds us that developing moral judgment takes time, effort, and guidance and encouragement from parents. She suggests these guidelines:

- *Relate to your child one-on-one.* Remember, teens often tune out when we lecture and nag.

- *Create conversation often by asking questions and listening.* Make it safe for your teen to have different views and to disagree.

- *Together establish clear standards* and a system of enforcement and consequences.

- *Make decisions for your child at crucial times,* without negotiating. When those occasions arise, we should emphasize our role as a guide in learning to assess risks and make appropriate decisions.

- *Affirm the positive choices and decisions your child makes.* We can show appreciation when our child lives up to expectations.

- *Take a firm stand against alcohol and drug use.*

- *Negotiate some rules when your child demonstrates good decision-making.* As parents we need to be flexible and give more freedom, flexibility or privileges when it is appropriate.

Self-regulation is learned

"Self-regulation involves behavior such as compliance, delay of gratification, and control of impulses," writes Rhoda Baruch, Ed.D., Chair of the Board at Institute of Mental Health Initiatives in Washington, D.C. One of our jobs as parents is to teach our children to make constructive, confident decisions when confronted with potentially dangerous situations. One way they learn self-regulation skills is when we give them questions to consider:

- What are the good things that might happen and the bad things that might happen?

- When you hear, "Everybody does it" or "We won't get caught" does that mean it's okay?

- Be honest with yourself and ask, "Is this the right thing to do?"

- Are you going to avoid trouble or take the risk and face the consequences?

- Consider what effect your behavior will have on other people? "What will my parents think?" "What would my grandparents think?"

- Be brave and feel confident when you make a wise decision.

When the pressure is on

When kids decide against taking a risk that might get them in trouble, it can discourage others from going ahead. We need to remind our child that he can decide who will make the decision. Our children must know that they have power to influence others. Point out that sometimes no one in the group really wants to take the risk, and if just one person says, "Wait a minute," others are likely to express reservations too. His good judgment can override the excitement of the moment.

And it literally can be a moment. "Kids sometimes have less than a minute to decide whether they're going to say yes or no," says a Northern Virginia middle school teacher, trained in peer pressure reversal. While you want to keep reinforcing what is "right," it is also important to talk about what to do when the pressure is really on, when there is a real threat. We can solicit suggestions from our child and give him our ideas:

When the pressure's on, what are the options? Leave the scene, ignore the person, change the subject, make a joke, act shocked, flatter the other person or come up with a better idea. Give your child permission to blame you–an especially good ploy to use quickly.

When your friends won't listen, and you feel really stuck or scared. Throw their keys in the bushes, pretend you are sick, call a taxi.

Common situations

We can help prepare our children for the common, everyday temptations they will face. When they work through scenarios until they are comfortable, they can confidently and rapidly respond to prompts like:

- "Just get in! I haven't had much to drink. We're not going far."
- "Slip these CDs in your pocket for me and walk out. No one will know."
- "My parents aren't home and some people are here. Why don't you come over?"
- "One puff won't hurt you!"
- "I used this paper last year with a different teacher. Your teacher will never recognize it."
- "Isn't that your mom's wallet? Just take the money for the earrings. She'll never miss it."

Enjoy reversing parts as you role-play with your teen. You'll both learn a lot!

Parents as models

Our children will follow our lead. We shouldn't expect them to exercise good judgment if we can't demonstrate it ourselves. If we drink and drive, tell white lies, and stay out late without checking in, so will they. Respecting our choices, and seeing us struggle with choices just as they do, will reinforce their own powers in making strong decisions.

Resisting risk-taking does not evolve in a smooth, linear fashion. Developing the ability to evaluate options, consider consequences and modulate impulses takes time and practice. Most importantly, we have to give our children guidance and values within a framework of love, support and encouragement.

Guidelines just for teens...resisting temptations

- Don't be impulsive.
- Evaluate the risks and consequences.
- Substitute positive goals for less desirable activities.
- Expect to be anxious; anxiety is normal.
- Learn to live with frustration. Don't give up after small defeats.
- Show strength; don't give in to peer pressures.
- Consider others who will be affected by your behavior.
- Delay and find other outlets for the group's energy.
- Keep informed about risks.
- Make decisions for yourself.
- Remember, others can take your positive lead.
- Resist temptations because your parents love you so much and want you to be safe.

See also: Alcohol, Cheating, Communicating, Dating, Parties, Sexual Responsibility, Shoplifting , Vandalism, Yes!

RESOURCES

The Romance of Risk: Why Teenagers Do the Things They Do. Lynn Ponton, Basic Books, 1997.

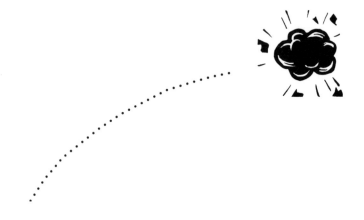

School Rivalry

Recently, uninvited teens drinking and loitering outside a McLean home where a party was being held took out baseball bats and damaged the car of a student from a rival school. In another incident, students attending an unchaperoned house party in Rockville were attacked and beaten by older students from a rival school. In yet another, a Washington family's car window was smashed in the middle of the night by a student from another school who professed to have no idea why he did it. These are unlawful acts.

A very small number of students harbor an irrational, deep-seated animosity toward other schools, and by extension, any students who attend them. Interestingly enough, these boys and girls are frequently not the athletes themselves, but the hangers-on, the wannabes, the attention-seekers who are the most vocal and most at risk of causing trouble between students at different schools, invariably outside of school hours and apart from school-sanctioned events. Party-crashing, brawling, and the destruction of personal property are decidedly unhealthy, and unlawful.

School spirit vs animosity

Every student wants to be proud of his or her school. Competition between schools, whether centered around academic, athletic, or artistic endeavors, is normal and healthy. Interestingly, almost all incidents of out-of-hand rivalry are related to athletic competitions. Results of academic and artistic competitions do not generate the same emotional intensity. (Strong athletic rivalries that go back decades, fierce competition on the playing field, and strong school spirit are all positive and healthy.)

Parents need to be able to differentiate between school spirit and traditional athletic rivalries on the one hand, and animosity and the potential for violence on the other. We need to make sure that our sons and daughters know the difference, too. They are, after all, our responsibility.

Good athletes play by the rules and play to win to bring honor to their school, to their teammates, and to themselves. Being proud of one's school and playing one's heart out on the athletic field, or cheering loudly from the grandstands for friends and school alike, are important parts of character development, team building, and school spirit. Fortunately, most athletes and spectators feel and act this way.

The principal point for parents and teens to keep in mind about full-contact sports such as football, hockey or lacrosse is that the students are playing a game. The game of football, for example, has a strict set of rules that must be followed by the players. There is a full complement of officials to enforce the rules on every play. There are physical limits to the playing field–sidelines and end zones. There are time limits to the game. The players are well-protected by padding and helmets. Yes, football is a rough sport because the players block and tackle one another at full speed. It's the nature of the game.

But good athletes and good fans also leave the struggle on the playing field after the final whistle has blown. After the game, the athletes themselves shake hands and look forward to doing it all over again next year. The fans, of course, should do likewise.

Parents should neither deny nor diminish their child's disapointment over losing. Acknowledge that it does feel bad to lose. Help your child find time and outlets for venting any anger. Don't tolerate threats by your child or among his teammates or classmates of "getting even" or punishing the other school or team. If your child seems unable to let go of his anger over hours or days, carefully appraise the level of hostility. Prevention is the key. Be clear that no incidence of vandalism or reprisal will be tolerated.

Tell your child never to assume that if unlawful acts occur, a grown-up with the right "connections" can "fix" things. This is almost always untrue and always unwise. When we teach our children responsibility, we must include responsibility for their actions.

Students who compete fiercely on the playing field are playing a game; students who engage in violence off the playing field are breaking the law.

See also: Alcohol, Anger, Parties, Harassment, Respect for Diversity, Risky Business, Sports, Vandalism

Sexual Responsibility

*Remember when sexual behavior was discussed in sports terms?
"I got to second base." These days the focus is, unfortunately, most
strongly on the "home run," i.e., intercourse.*

Our children's choice of favorite music, film stars, and TV shows
is, of course, very much affected by their peers. So are their attitudes
toward sex. Those attitudes often reflect misinformation which has
passed from one teenager to another.

As parents, this developmental reality should empower us to
clarify and discuss our values and views about sexuality and sexual
responsibility with our children. While we discuss the clear and
present dangers of unprotected sexual intercourse, the complications
of unwanted pregnancy, the life-and-death issues of sexually transmitted disease including AIDS, and the availability of condoms, we
frequently overlook the issues of relationships and love. Affectionate
behaviors like hand-holding, necking and petting are seldom included in our discussions, even though they are important and for-
mative experiences.

However, if we have fostered a trusting relationship with our
children, we may be able to talk intimately about all the things that

are part of a sexual relationship. About how we hope they will not be influenced by peer pressure to become sexually involved. About how we hope they will first have closeness and friendship. Our children sometimes surprise us with their openness.

Talking about s-e-x

As parents we are the best judge of when, how and what sexual information to share with our children. Forget about what Calvin Klein has to say, or Pepsi, or the characters on "Beverly Hills 90210." They don't know our children as well as we do nor do they know how our children process relevant information.

Waiting for just the right moment to bring up sexuality may put our children's health and lives at greater risk. We need to start early in our children's lives, recognizing that sexual desire is a normal and healthy part of growing up. Every parent expects that his child will become sexually involved sometime in his life. We hope these experiences will be satisfying and enjoyable for them. We just want it—especially sexual intercourse—to be later, maybe a lot later. Life is filled with "teachable moments" to establish and reinforce our values and the "facts." Now is the time for us as parents to start talking to our children about becoming responsible sexual persons.

We want our children to enjoy their youth, be popular and increasingly mature. And to do so, may mean they face a familiar form of peer pressure and acceptance—to become sexually active, often to the extent of having intercourse. A recent survey conducted at a local middle school revealed that 65 percent of 12- and 13-year-olds polled feel a lot of sexual pressure. In a similar study conducted in the metropolitan Washington area on a randomly selected group of teenagers, ages 12 to 17, 61 percent of the boys and 76 percent of the girls reported that they are under too much pressure to have sexual intercourse. This same survey revealed that more than 64 percent of the boys and 43 percent of the girls believe that it is either somewhat important or very important to have a steady boyfriend or girlfriend.

According to the Centers for Disease Control and Prevention (CDCP), sexually transmitted diseases infect between 2.5 million and 3 million teenagers annually. By age 21, one in four young people is already infected with a sexually transmitted disease such as chlamydia, syphilis, gonorrhea, herpes, or genital warts.

Teens talk

Teens who are willing to share their experiences say that they regularly engage in sexual behaviors at home while their parents are asleep or away, and they frequently engage in impromptu encounters at small parties rife with alcohol and other drugs. They say their sexual activity is a natural response to a sex-saturated society and to crushing peer pressure. Many medical specialists and counselors confirm that teenagers are becoming sexually active at younger and younger ages. Moreover, they report having more short term, consecutive partners. A nationwide CDCP survey found that 40 percent of teenagers polled said they had had sexual intercourse by the ninth grade and that nearly 20 percent had had four or more sexual partners during the year of the study. Sexual activity among youth crosses all racial, religious and socio-economic boundaries and lifestyle orientations.

Among the teens who speak out, some tell us that they view sex as a recreational sport filled with the thrills of conquest and entertainment. It's fun. It makes them appear more mature to their peers. It's a means of rehearsing for adulthood. It provides an element of control and an opportunity to defy the odds and parental authority. Adolescent specialists warn us that teens who are involved in sexual intercourse are potential victims of psychological distress, abuse, disease and even death.

Patrick F. Bassett, President of the Independent School Association of the Central States, observes that since the physical, emotional and psychological dangers of early intercourse increase as one goes down the age scale (i.e., the younger you start, the more likely you are to have multiple partners and increased risks), a decision to abstain or postpone sexual intercourse is both wise and deserving of support.

Who's responsible?

Many parents have depended on their communities–schools, churches and youth groups–to educate their children about sex and sexual responsibility. Programs run the gamut from preaching total abstinence to dispensing condoms and other forms of protection. Sometimes the information that community-based programs give children seems to conflict with their parents' values regarding sexual behavior and responsibility. When families and schools work together, emphasizing shared values along with sound decision-making skills and accurate information, teenagers are well-served and behave more responsibly.

Parents are faced with a formidable challenge to bridge the gap between the messages that our children receive from mass media and their peers. Our children need information that is accurate, reliable, honest and compassionate. They need information that touches their hearts as well as their minds. "Hard, cold facts" like the changes a prepubescent child goes through in preparation for adulthood is a major contrast to the "warm, fuzzy, touchy-feely facts" on such issues as the emotional rollercoaster one experiences when sexually aroused. Children need to understand not only the characteristics of a healthy sexual experience but also those of an abusive sexual relationship. They need to know about the joys of love and intimacy but also about handling rejection and disappointment from failed relationships.

The goal is to prepare our children for future changes in their sexual interest, expectations and perceptions and to help them develop a positive attitude about their sexuality. What our kids need most, counsels human sexuality educator Deborah Roffman, is more discussion of moral values with their parents. Teens do want adults' views on values–more than they want more discussions about the dangers of early sexual activity and best forms of contraception.

Parents talk

Before opening up the channels of communication with our child regarding sexual behavior and responsibility, we will need to open up that baggage containing our own sexual experiences, views, opinions, values, expectations, disappointment and joys. What kinds of sexual experiences are appropriate before marriage? What are our views on homosexuality? Do TV, music and movies realistically depict sexual intimacy? How would we respond if our child told us that she did not believe in monogamous relationships? The goal here is not to have all of the answers nor to anticipate all of the questions, but to prepare ourselves to explore together with our children uncharted regions of their sexual sensitivity and curiosity.

To talk openly and freely about sexuality, we have to be in tune with our own perceptions of the subject. Reflection, introspection, acceptance and honest, compassionate expression are the responses which will best help our child. If necessary, professional counseling may help overcome any anxiety which interferes with our ability to communicate effectively. If this discussion with our child will be shared with another significant adult, then both grown-ups must understand each other's sexual viewpoints so that if there are differences, they will be presented as rational differences rather than disagreements.

It is not advisable to share explicit details of our personal sexual experiences with our child since the goal is to be a parent, counselor and supporter, not a peer. Relating our experiences as a teenager—feelings of disappointment, confusion, loneliness—can be discussed appropriately with a 13-year-old who seems fascinated about sex, without describing actual sexual experiences. Likewise, sharing the fears and possible outcomes of date-rape can be done without sharing explicit, personal experiences of this kind.

As a parent, we have a responsibility to share our values and rationale with our child. If having multiple partners is not acceptable to us, we can put this value in some context which our child can understand. If our behavior does not mirror our values, then our child needs to know our reasoning for this dissonance. For example, a daughter may witness that her divorced mother has more than one sexual partner, and ask why she can't do likewise. Do we tell her simply that it's okay for adults to behave like this, but not young people; or, do we carefully talk through the complex issues and dynamics involved?

Similarly, in sharing our values with our child, we need to also share our expectations. If it is our expectation for our child to remain a virgin until after he graduates from high school, then say so. This might prompt the teen to share his reasoning for having expectations that are similar to or different from ours.

A hallmark of this kind of discussion is careful listening—we need to remember to allow our child to do some of the talking. In addition to providing accurate, reliable, honest information, our goal is to better understand our child and the challenges she is facing. Non-judgmental, compassionate listening is the way we can best accomplish this. On occasions when our child seems disinterested in talking to us, we can let him know that we will be available to pick up the discussion at another time. In fact, talking about sexuality is not something we can schedule, but is best touched upon many times as the opportunity rises. Often the behavior of a sit-com character or the way a passerby is draped over and around their date can initiate a conversation about sex. The child might make a casual comment. We might follow with an open-ended response. A conversation begins.

If we find (or suspect) that our son or daughter is engaging in risky behaviors—like having unprotected sexual intercourse, sex while under the influence of alcohol or drugs, or being sexually violent—immediate, direct and compassionate dialogue is called for. We could preface our remarks with statements expressing our concerns and fears about the risky behavior. By enlisting our child's input, together we can tackle the problem of his or her safety. We can introduce or stress alternative behaviors which will minimize the risk. Perhaps this child will need additional support from counseling professionals.

For many parents, talking about sexuality is not easy. It requires the willingness to bring up sensitive and potentially embarrassing subjects like masturbation, sexual orientation and physical intimacy. Knowing how difficult it can be will help us understand our child's reluctance to broach the subject. Our responsibility as a parent is to take the lead. The best way is to communicate with our children, helping them to appreciate that sexual choices involve many consequences. When we initiate the dialogue, our child will have the benefit of another point of view—ours!

See also: Alone, Dating, Date Rape, Gender, Risky Business

RESOURCES

Choices or Chances—Deciding About Sex, Mary Joe Nolin. 1990.

Everybody's Doing It!: How to Survive Your Teenagers' Sex Life (and Help Them Survive It Too), Andrea Warren and Jay Wiedenkeller, New York: Penguin. 1993.

The First Time: Women Speak Out About Losing Their Virginity, Karen Bouris. Berkeley, CA: Conari Press. 1993.

If This Is Love, Why Do I Feel So Insecure?, C. Hindy, J. C. Schwartz, and A. Brodsky New York: Fawcett Crest. 1989.

Losing It: The Virginity Myth, edited by Louis M. Crosier. Washington, DC: Avocus. 1993.

Promiscuities: The Secret Struggle for Womanhood, Naomi Wolf.
New York, NY: Random House. 1997.

Raising A Child Conservatively in a Sexually Permissive World, Sol Gordon
and Judith Gordon. Fireside Books. 1983.

Reviving Ophelia: Saving the Lives of Adolescent Girls, Mary Pipher.
New York, NY: Ballantine Books. 1994.

Sex and Love: What's a Teenager to Do? Mary Beth Bonacci. A videotape
distributed by Gateway Films/Vision Video. 1995.

Straight From the Heart: How to Talk to Your Teenagers About Love and Sex,
Carol Cassell. New York, NY: Simon and Schuster. 1987.

What's Happening to My Body?: For Boys, Linda Madaras. New York, NY:
New Market Press. 1987.

What's Happening to My Body?: For Girls, Linda Madaras. New York, NY:
New Market Press. 1988.

You and Your Adolescent: A Parent's Guide for Ages 10–20, Laurence
Steinberg & Ann Levine. New York, NY: Harper Perennial. 1990.

Community Resources

Parent Encouragement Program (PEP) offers classes in Fostering Healthy
Sexual Development in Children. Call 301-929-8824 for more information.

The Education Department of Planned Parenthood provides speakers
by request on topics such as "Talking with Your Children about Sex."
For more information, call 202-347-8500.

Organizations

Campaign for Our Children, Inc., is a nonprofit abstinence-based teen pregnancy prevention program aimed at pre-sexually active children between the
ages of 9 and 14. 410-576-9000 or www.cfoc.org

Sexuality Information and Education Council of the United States, SIECUS, is
a nonprofit organization which affirms that sexuality is a natural healthy part
of living. It develops, collects and disseminates information and advocates for
the right to make responsible sexual choices. 212-819-9770 or
www.siecus.org

Shoplifting = Stealing!

$\int$ hoplifting is risky business! Parents of shoplifters feel afraid, outraged, and embarrassed. One Chevy Chase mother recently found new, tagged clothing in her daughter's room that had obviously been stolen from a local store. She confronted her daughter, and when the teenager admitted stealing, the mother said, "Cut off the tags, throw everything in the washer, and never tell anyone you did this!"

What happens when a juvenile is caught shoplifting? How does shoplifting affect the family and friends of the shoplifter? Will the school get involved? Can shoplifting lead to more serious crimes?

It's a crime

Shoplifting is a crime in all our local jurisdictions. Shoplifting affects merchandise prices as merchants add the cost of losses and prosecutions to the prices of goods and services. Police in Fairfax County say that individual merchants handle cases as they see fit; most merchants at the county's Springfield Mall report that they prosecute in virtually every case. Detection devices are more numerous and sophisticated and plain clothes security is more plentiful. Mom and pop stores have given way to large chains with the money, time and staff to see that prosecutions do take place.

The legal repercussions do not always reflect the size or value of the stolen item. Parents should be aware that their children will probably be stopped initially by security guards, not the police, and that these guards are not always interested in the legal rights of the shoplifter. Reports from around the country suggest that security guards do not always feel obligated to follow proper procedures when apprehending suspected shoplifters. Once turned over to the police, shoplifters are tried in juvenile court and convictions carry sentences that range from probation to community service, to juvenile detention, or some combination of the above.

In addition, heads of local independent schools feel that student actions (even those which occur off-campus) can have a negative impact on the school community and they often discipline students. Honor codes at some schools are used to further discipline students who break the rules outside of school. Convictions, even in juvenile court, may follow a child into adulthood and affect college and job opportunities.

This is an issue that calls for forethought, guidelines and rules before there is a problem. Talk to your child about the consequences and repercussions of shoplifting. Let your child know your feelings about stealing. Make sure your child knows that a person in the company of a shoplifter may suffer the same penalties as the shoplifter. Psychologists recommend that if you discover your child has stolen items, that he should always make restitution as well as receive some additional penalty such as completing an unpleasant chore or losing a valued privilege.

Children who steal

- Very young children take things that excite interest.
- Older children may steal if they feel a sibling is favored.
- Some may steal to show bravery to friends.
- Others may steal to give presents and be more popular.
- A few children take what they need out of a fear of dependency.
- Some may steal to get attention from (express anger or get even with) parents.

Professional treatment may be necessary if a child steals persistently. Sociologists report that children who have engaged in minor delinquencies as adolescents are 26 times as likely to commit serious crimes as children who have not. They are twice as likely to have some mental health problems and three times as likely to use marijuana.

To prevent children from shoplifting or from progressing from shoplifting to more serious crimes:

- *Give children clear expectations* for their behavior, including that stealing (even small items) will not be tolerated.
- *Monitor behavior*–know what your children are doing, who they're with, and where they are.
- *Review receipts* for all purchases they make in the context of budgeting and practical shopping skills.
- *Teach your child how to save* for desired purchases and discuss the need to delay gratification.

Discuss with your child:

- Your expectations concerning behavior in stores.
- "Guilt by association;" if another child steals, your child may be blamed too.
- Getting a "special discounted price" from a friend working in a store is stealing unless sanctioned by the manager or owner.
- Their response if a friend shoplifts.
- Their behavior if stopped by a security guard or police.

Signs of shoplifting

Montgomery County police suggest that parents look for the following warnings:

- Finding store tags or package wrappings hidden in the trash.
- Noticing your child wearing baggy clothing, when it is not his usual attire, or wearing a jacket when it is warm.
- Noticing your child's new clothing, jewelry, or other items you did not purchase/your child could not afford to purchase.
- Seeing your child frequently carrying a large empty purse or backpack when she leaves home.

See also: Cheating, Money, Shopping Malls, Risky Business, Vandalism

Shopping Malls: Today's Main Streets

"My son wants to "hang out" all day at the mall with his friends!" a 12- year-old's mother said. "He says all his friends will be there; there's nothing else to do; we don't live near enough to any of his friends so that he can get together with them easily; and last but not least, every other parent said it's okay." A phone check with other parents revealed that it wasn't all right with them and that they wanted their children to spend the day more productively. Another mother eating lunch with her 14 year-old son at the Union Station food court watched as a drug deal took place at the next table. Malls are kid magnets–the way the neighborhood vacant lot used to be.

The mall is the place to "see and be seen" by peers. Independent school children often live far away from their school friends, so the mall becomes a place to meet that is convenient for all. They can shop, eat, play video games, watch a movie, and catch up with "the latest" and, protected from the elements, walk around and look good. Teenagers are cruising mall corridors as young people once cruised the main streets of a small town.

Trouble

The trouble kids get into at malls has led some local mall managers to implement strict new rules for youth under the age of 18. At Springfield Mall group size is limited and behavior is closely monitored. In addition, police substations have been established at Springfield Mall and Montgomery Mall and increased uniformed security is present. Mall managers say that large groups of teenagers discourage other shoppers and disrupt businesses. On the other hand, teenagers have more money than ever to spend and seem to prefer to be in groups when they spend it.

Kids alone in a mall may be vulnerable; kids in groups can get into trouble that would never occur with parental supervision. The increase in police and security guards in malls may lead parents to believe that malls are a safe place for their children to meet. This is not necessarily the case. Shoplifting by teens is much more prevalent than crimes committed against children. However, increased police presence is a result of more crime in general occurring in the mall areas. Several well publicized car-jackings and robberies in local malls have raised public awareness of some of the problems.

Will your child find trouble or will trouble find your child at the mall? The answer lies in parental preparation before the problem arises. A child with a purpose to be at the mall is more likely to have a safe and satisfying visit and less likely to encounter problems. Planning, preparation, and communication with your child and other parents can lead to greater maturity and independence for your child. The following may help clarify the rules for visits.

Discuss with your child:

- Expectations for behavior, including courtesy toward others and surroundings.
- Concerns for safety.
- Transportation, time limits, and meeting place.
- "Guilt by association," your child may be blamed too when another child does something wrong.
- How to get help if a problem arises, i.e., approaches by strangers, broken merchandise, shoplifting.
- Malls have a purpose–selling things–so don't do anything to impede that purpose.

- Never leave the mall with anyone except the previously agreed upon person.
- What would you do if a friend shoplifted?
- What would you do if approached by a security guard?

Mall visits should have a purpose, a time limit, and an agreed upon meeting place. At least one parent should be within phone contact if a problem should occur and all the children in the group should have the number where that parent can be reached. Let your child know that you will "be there for him" no matter what kind of problem should occur.

For younger kids, 10 to 12 years old

If you allow your younger child to go to malls, consider the following:

- Establish a time limit, which may be as short as an hour.
- Have one parent who will be nearby shopping.
- Establish a known meeting place.
- Make sure kids know your plans.
- Tell your child how to have you paged at the mall.
- Help your child (and friends) develop a shopping plan.

Rules for kids
- Go to a mall with a least one friend–only during the daytime.
- Stay together at all times.
- Plan ahead of time what to do if you get separated.
- Never go to the bathroom or sit in a movie alone.

See also: Alone, Money, Risky Business, Shoplifting, Vandalism

Smoking

Smoking is a matter of life and death. Many teenagers don't see it that way. In fact, three thousand teens begin smoking every day. (Tobacco is responsible for the deaths of 450,000 Americans every year–more than alcohol, cocaine, crack, heroin, murder, suicide, car accidents, fire, and AIDS combined.) For parents, the most troubling truth in the tobacco statistics is that nearly all of those smokers began their habit as children. Every single year during the '90s, the numbers of children who smoke have increased, to nearly 30 percent in 1996. Tragically, one in three of them will die as a result of their poor choice in childhood. Former Food and Drug Administration (FDA) Commissioner David Kessler has changed the way policy makers think about tobacco by calling smoking "a pediatric disease." Illness and death may occur in adulthood but it is children who become addicted.

Risk taking

The tobacco industry insists that smoking is an adult choice. And parents themselves might reasonably discount the seriousness of smoking by thinking their child can quit later, when maturity and wisdom kick in. However, the reality of nicotine addiction imposes real limitations on those who try. Four out of five teen smokers have tried to quit but few succeed. Seventy percent of teens who smoke say they wouldn't start if they had it to do over again. And 17 million adult smokers per year try to quit, yet only 10 percent succeed. These are sobering facts for parents who know they must choose their battles carefully during years characterized by experimenting and risk-taking.

Ironically, nearly all children under 10 have intensely negative opinions about smoking. Ask, and they are happy to tell you with a grimace, "smoking is stupid...smoking is disgusting...smoking can kill you...I would *never* smoke." However, something happens to many of these kids as they reach their middle school years. The average smoker tried that first cigarette around 13 years old and was a daily smoker by 14. What happens between 9 and 13? And what can parents do to keep their children healthy and tobacco-free?

As parents (and former teenagers ourselves), we all know that adolescence, by its nature, is a period of experimenting with risky behavior, stretching one's limits, and drawing a wider line between the child and the parent. These attitudes and behaviors are clearly the normal developmental path to adulthood. Our role as parents is to help our children arrive at adulthood as effective self-advocates, able to make good choices on their own behalf. In the interim, one of the problems parents face is that teens tend to be a bit irrational about risks in general.

An 8-year-old might be very able to articulate that cigarettes are addictive and dangerous. (The Environmental Protection Agency in fact has rated nicotine as a Class A carcinogen, in the same category as asbestos. The National Institute of Child Health & Human Development has found that smoking impairs fertility and increases likelihood of irregular menstrual cycles.) But the average teen, as discovered in numerous studies, seems much less clear–either underestimating or unaware of nicotine's health risks and addictive potential. However, it is harder for teens to get cigarettes since February 1997 when FDA regulations made it unlawful to sell tobacco products to anyone under 18.

Smoking can be a red flag

Characteristics of adolescence which can change a passionate 9-year-old anti-smoker into a 15-year-old smoker include peer pressure, rebellion, academic failure, anxiety and depression. For girls, the desire to be thin can be a contributing factor. Smoking can be part of an array of behaviors that include eating disorders. Making the choice to smoke can be a red flag, warning parents of low self-esteem. Dr. Sharon Stoliaroff, a Chevy Chase clinical psychologist, notes that "teen smoking is ultimately a willingness to engage in self-destructive behavior." While rebellion and peer influence may be ordinary consequences of adolescence, they don't necessarily result in unhealthy choices. A teenager can rebel without smoking. Connections can be made with non-smoking peers since 70 percent of teens don't smoke.

Knowing that smoking might be a sign of trouble can transform a parent's reaction from anger and hostility to one of compassion, helpfulness, and understanding. Only a few of our teenagers smoke just to get a rise out of us. Very likely the problem runs deeper and the child could use some help. The way we respond will depend on our parenting style, our attitudes about smoking, and our child's age and personality. Although parents may sometimes feel helpless in their struggle with adolescent behavior, studies have shown that *parents have much more influence than they realize.* This can be a very reassuring assumption.

Prevention is best

- First, cigarette smoking deserves to be treated as a serious problem because of the addictive potential of nicotine. Parents need to guard against the ostrich-problem of ignoring their hunches in order to avoid a conflict. By the time the problem is recognized, the child's power to choose to quit can be greatly diminished by the force of addiction.

- If a parent smokes, that behavior should be examined. Having a parent who smokes greatly increases the likelihood that a child will smoke.

- Help kids find outside activities that they like to do. Kids who enjoy being good at something are a step ahead in their self-esteem. Sports are especially good at giving kids respect for their bodies. If your child is not successful at traditional sports, try off-the-beaten-path options like karate, yoga, or rock climbing. Talent in music, the arts, math and the sciences, outdoor skills like hiking or orienteering, or games like chess are all fertile fields to develop.

- Peer pressure is enormously important. Getting a teen or, a preteen involved in a supportive interest/activity group can be pivotal. Scouts, rock-climbing or computer clubs, candy stripers, youth orchestras or jazz ensembles or any local service group are places where teens can feel important, useful and successful among similar peers.

- Try to ensure that your child's money (which most likely comes from a parent in the form of allowance or spending money) is not used for cigarettes, by discussing the cumulative dollar costs of smoking and your child's weekly or long-range financial planning.

- Petition your child's school to be smoke-free if it isn't already. Teachers who smoke give the wrong message to kids. Schools should be leaders in public health.

- Encourage other adolescents and young adults to speak to kids about smoking. Having parents' opinions validated by peers is very helpful.

- Make sure that parents feel free to network. Our neighborhoods extend beyond where we live to include the larger school and religious communities. Most parents would appreciate knowing if another parent spotted their child smoking.

- Support politicians who favor restrictions on advertising aimed at young people and youth access to tobacco. It is little surprise that 85 percent of adolescents who smoke buy the three most heavily advertised brands.

Helping a child to quit

If you suspect your child is smoking, "…engage in a dialogue, not a battle," suggests Dr. Stoliaroff. How parents approach a problem with an adolescent has everything to do with how successful they are likely to be. Your attitude can help your teen build confidence in himself as a reasonable person and his trust in you as a compassionate advocate. Dr. Stoliaroff recommends that parents:

- Listen thoughtfully and respectfully, without an agenda.

- Understand what smoking means to your child, how it started, why it continues.

- Respond to underlying self-esteem issues with alternative coping strategies and therapy if necessary.

- Express pride and confidence in your child's effort to quit, even in the face of setbacks.

- Be patient, optimistic and encouraging.

- Set appropriate limits. For example, cigarette smoking is not permitted in your home, car, or in your presence.

According to some experts, young love can be a great motivator. Kids respond to the fact that bad breath, smelly clothes, yellow teeth, and a hacking cough are a major turn-off to the opposite sex. When all else fails, cupid may be the best ally.

See also: Alcohol, Communicating, Eating, Risky Business, Stress

RESOURCES

Ad Libbing It. A humorous video for 6th–8th graders which critiques alcohol and cigarette advertising. Robert Jaffe of Doctors Ought to Care. Call 800-323-9084.

The Advocacy Institute. Produces a monthly newsletter with tips and resources for advocacy, $50/year. Phone: 202-659-8475, or write: 1707 L Street NW, Suite 400, Washington, DC 20036.

Campaign for Tobacco-Free Kids. A source for information, resources and support. Offers an Action Kit–a free packet containing information about kids and tobacco for the tobacco control advocate. Call 1-800-284-KIDS.

Centers for Disease Control and Prevention. *Jam.* A magazine for young adults. Discusses drinking and tobacco use. *Jam* video, a supplement to "Jam" magazine. For a free sample call 800-CDC-1311 and select "promotional offer."

Cigarettes, Cigarettes. The Dirty Rotten Truth About Tobacco. An illustrated, paperback for kids about the risks of tobacco. Pete Traynor for Sights Productions. 1993. Phone: 410-795-4582 or write: 15130 Black Ankle Road, Mt. Airy, MD 21771.

Food and Drug Administration's Regulations making it unlawful to sell tobacco products to minors: 888-FDA-4KIDS or www.fda.gov

Institute of Medicine for National Academy Press. *Growing up Tobacco Free.* A handbook discussing tobacco and addiction in children. 1994. $24. Phone: 800-624-6242 or 202-334-3313 or write: 2101 Constitution Avenue NW, Box 285, Washington DC 20055.

Kids Say Don't Smoke. A book encouraging kids not to start smoking. Andrew Tobias. New York: Workman Publishing. 800-722-7202 or write: 708 Broadway, 6th floor, New York, NY 10003.

The Lesko Brothers' Web Page. The Lesko brothers, ages 6 and 9 explain the proposed FDA regulations and the problem of easy access to tobacco. www.cquest.com/leskobrothers.html

Maryland Cancer Control Plan. Hotline to provide information about tobacco cessation programs. 800-477-9774.

SGR 4 Kids. A supplement to the 1994 Surgeon General's Report, for 5th and 6th graders. Both publications available at 800-CDC-1311 or write: Office on Smoking and Health, Mail Stop K-50, Atlanta, GA 30333.

STAT– Stop Teenage Addiction to Tobacco. Publishes a newsletter, manuals, guides and products aimed at preventing tobacco industry's access to young people. 121 Lyman Street, Suite 120, Springfield, MA 01103.

Sorrow: Coping with Loss

ometimes school communities must face up to the unthinkable: young people aren't supposed to die. Teachers aren't supposed to die. Parents aren't supposed to die. But they do. Sometimes accidentally, sometimes because of illness, sometimes violently, sometimes by suicide. The results of any tragedy will affect a school community profoundly. How can parents help their children, themselves and their community to cope if tragedy strikes?

School counselors, administrators, and bereavement experts say the first step is to be educated about the dangers facing young people, especially the increasing risks of violent acts and suicides. Homicides now top the list of reasons why young people die, with accidents coming second and suicides ranked closely behind. Experts point out that the suicide rate actually may be higher because many young people who are determined to commit suicide intentionally crash their cars to kill themselves.

Especially for teenagers, the suicide statistics are very sobering. According to the National Center for Health Statistics, the rate at which teenagers are taking their own lives has tripled since 1960. And for every successful suicide, there are 50 to 100 adolescent suicide attempts. Each year, about 250,000 teenagers in the U.S. attempt suicide, and 35,000 of them succeed. That's about 50 a week. More boys succeed than girls, generally because their methods are more violent.

What can parents do?

The most important thing parents can do is to talk and to listen. Ellen Sanford, a local bereavement counselor working with children, emphasizes that communication is key in helping both to prevent tragedies and to ease the pain of those who have suffered a loss. Especially with adolescents, she said, acknowledging sadness is vital. "The pressures young people face during adolescence are greater than in any other time of human development," she said. "But sometimes parents get so used to the ups and downs of mood swings that they don't pay attention."

Experts agree that depression and suicidal thoughts are closely linked. Everyone who deals with a depressed child–parents, teachers, counselors and administrators and especially peers–needs to take every threat of suicide seriously. "There is a myth that if they do talk about it, they won't do it," Sanford said. "But the fact is that 80 percent of those who talk about suicide actually do try it."

Serious warning signs of an adolescent contemplating suicide usually include "feeling rotten inside" and threats such as "I won't be a bother to you much longer." Parents also should be very concerned when a troubled child begins cleaning his or her room or giving away cherished possessions like a CD collection or experiences a sudden change of mood and begins to feel euphoric. You need to get help, to get them talking to counselors and to peers. Make an appointment for the two of you; tell her it's important to you that she give a counselor a try. Convince her that the therapist is no scarier than the guidance counselor at school.

Kids who are thinking about suicide need someone who will reassure them not to be afraid of their thoughts. "The saddest cases are those who feel that there is no hope and that no one loves them. Someone needs to be able to say, 'I care if you die, even if you don't think anyone else does.

"Even if you think to yourself, 'Oh, that's just a joke–he doesn't really mean it,' you still have to take it seriously," concurred Fr. Peter Weigand, O.S.B., headmaster of a boys' school where the suicide of a popular and highly successful high school junior stunned the school community in 1997. "We missed it in this case because the young man was doing so well academically and everything seemed to be going so smoothly. But sometimes those are the very kids schools miss–the overachievers who feel lost inside. It seems odd because you'd never think anything was wrong. Everything they touch seems to turn to gold. But what's going on inside, you just don't know."

Whatever the cause of the death, parents should support their child's desire to attend the funeral or memorial service. This can be an important event for teens who may rely on peers more than parents to deal with the loss. Often, boys as well as girls weep openly and lean on each other at such services, finding some comfort. Later they can celebrate the memory of one who is gone as well as their own young lives.

How do schools confront a tragic event?

Crisis counseling is vital when death touches a school because everyone needs to have a chance to express their grief. Several organizations in the greater Washington area have trained counselors available who will come to the school immediately and help the community through the initial crisis. All schools should have a plan in place, experts agree. At the boys' school discussed earlier, more than a dozen crisis counselors arrived on-site within an hour of the time the school learned of the student's death. The school's guidance counselor was trained in crisis intervention and had worked at another school where an accident had taken the lives of a teacher and student. Students were counseled as a group and individually, and parents were notified. Counseling sessions also were held for the faculty and other adults in the community. An evening meeting was held for school parents to share their concerns.

One school community that lost a well-loved teacher to cancer, created an opportunity for children, parents, and staff to purchase recommended books to expand the school library. The list of books reflected the teacher's interests or were resource books about death and dying. Another school marked the death of a valued staff member by naming a new scholarship fund in her name. At another memorial service, the girlfriends of the deceased student wrote messages on balloons, which they released into the clearing skies. When a rainbow appeared, the girls "felt" the spirit of their departed friend. Other schools have planted a tree or a special garden in remembrance of a student or teacher who died. Many parents participated in these projects, confirming their child's need to express grief.

It takes time

Continuing recognition of loss and grief is an important consideration for school communities and for parents. And continuing to listen compassionately to those who have suffered is vital, Sanford said. Especially in dealing with children, it is important not to minimize their loss or to try to "make things all right." For example, telling a child, even a teenager, that her mother would rather be in heaven with grandma than with her is very hurtful. It's better to simply say that you are very sorry about what happened.

Don't shy away from those who have suffered a loss. Take the lead and create the opportunity to let them talk. Those who are grieving need a chance to tell their story over and over until they can accept it and grow through it. Parents and schools must remember that the process may take weeks, months and maybe even years to accept a loss. The loss is often felt more intensely at times such as birthdays or holidays, and survivors may go through periods when they are furious at the person who died and feel guilty for the fact that they are still living.

Such are the aftershocks of losses such as death, which Washington author Marguerite Kelly identified in her popular *Family Almanac* as "the earthquakes of the soul." "They shake the structure of your life and they never leave you quite as trusting as you were before," she said, but we can support our children by reminding them that "they can get through...with reasonable grace, not because other people have done it, but because, in a sense, you have been preparing for these upheavals all your life. Every time you handled a challenge well, you were teaching yourself to cope with these crises. You will survive, because you always have." We overcome our losses because there are people around us who care.

See also: Depression

RESOURCES

Center for Loss & Grief Therapy: (301) 942-6440
Individual therapy for grieving children, adolescents and adults. Provides training to schools, groups and colleges.

Children of Separation and Divorce Center: (C.O.S.D.)
Rockville (301) 384-0079, Columbia (410) 740-9553
Individual, family and group therapy on separation and divorce, as well as

other parenting issues. Parenting seminars on separation and divorce. Publications and professional training.

Holy Cross Hospice Bereavement Center: (301) 754-7742
Adult and children's support groups

Hospice of Northern Virginia: (703) 534-7070
Sponsors Camp Begin-Again, a summer camp program for children dealing with grief

Jewish Social Service Agency: (301) 881-3700
Bereaved parents support groups

Montgomery Hospice Society, Inc.: (301) 279-2566
Group sessions for adolescent loss, bereaved children, parental loss for adults, sudden loss, widowed persons, and pet loss.

St. Francis Center: (202) 333-4880
Child and adolescent programs for those dealing with all types of losses including death, trauma, divorce, chronic and life threatening illnesses. The Center offers individual, group and family counseling and play therapy. Provides education, support and community outreach to Washington area schools.

Sports: What's the Goal?

Why is it that some reasonable, calm parents suddenly blow a mental gasket at the sight of goalposts or bases, children, and a ball, demanding a win at all costs? Why do these lovely people go through personality changes on the sidelines of the sports field that would do Dr. Jekyll and Mr. Hyde proud? Why do some parents have such incredible expectations for their children?

Graham Ramsay, director of The Soccer School in Rockville says we can blame several factors, "…including a desire on the part of parents to become involved with every facet of their children's lives and the media's over-glorification of professional sports. What began as a genuine desire to help children and to share their experiences has spiraled downward into a contest for winning games and trophies, a contest aided and abetted by an extremely visible parent support system."

As parents we are the greatest influence on the youth sports scene. We can make or destroy athletics for our child. Perhaps the biggest challenge for us is to balance the need for our support with the tendency to become over-involved–especially emotionally. Our best intentions can produce negative behaviors detrimental to our child and the team as a whole.

Parents who are involved a lot and know the game are frequently a lot more tolerant of the action. They get satisfaction noting the subtlety of the plays, timing and strategies as well as an individual team member's skill development. Ramsay believes that parents who don't understand the sport, those who give opinions based on misconceptions, are frequently the parents who are most visibly and verbally critical from the sidelines.

Parents' role

As parents we should realize that the world of professional sports and the world of children are, at minimum, a million light-years apart. "This so-called 'winning mentality'," observes Ramsay, "often puts kids in the losing column as they opt out of sports to calmer pastures where they can make their own decisions without the constant baying of adult 'expertise'. Who can blame them? If those same parents were on the receiving end of the same verbal assault they would probably join the rest of the drop-outs...."

It is vital to maintain the priority of learning the basics well, both on the field or court and in life skills. Playing sports is about the development of a child, from acquiring skills in a sport to becoming a valued teammate: a real winning formula. To make this happen, we should help create a positive learning environment. This is especially true during and after competitions when emotions run high.

Actions do speak louder than words. Regardless of what we may preach to our children about "just have fun" and "it doesn't matter who wins or loses, but how you play the game," our reactions, and more importantly the intensity of our reactions, significantly affects our children. We all have witnessed the chilling effect of the parent who berates coaches, referees or players. Somehow the fun just goes out of the game and the play and players turn from spirited to grim.

The pressure to win inflicted upon children and teens (individually or in teams) closes the door on their development. "The fun of playing evaporates," observes Ramsay, "and is substituted by a bottom line mentality where fun can only be derived from winning. Young players need the freedom to experiment, to fail, to try again and again without the constant heat of competition scalding their errors." Acquiring a skill demands a deep commitment from the player and the self-motivation to practice over and over again. We cannot do it for our children but we can help them by providing consistent encouragement and being good role models.

Through our words and our example, we teach our children that you lose and you live and you move on. We have to acknowledge that losing is a part of what happens on the way to success.

Winning and losing

One of the problems with youth sports is that winning and losing get twisted to the point where they acquire a strange status. Ramsay observes, "Winning is equated as a form of excellence and losing is treated like a social disease. I feel players need to lose about 20 to 25 percent of their games in order to learn. In fact there's nothing wrong with losing if you have given your best. The loss can become a learning win as players know what to do to improve, including learning from their opponent's play."

If we go berserk with happiness when our child "scores" and are silent with depression or rabid with anger when she "fails," we may want to examine why our child's winning is so important. The parent or child who must always win is going to face many harsh disappointments; there will always be someone who will win more, earn more and achieve more than she will.

Personal growth

A purpose of sports is to help develop a character strong enough to deal productively with setbacks. Too often as parents we want our children to have pain-free learning experiences. When being dropped or losing is treated as someone else's fault, these isolated, protective reactions block our children's opportunity to deal with disappointment and to develop a stronger, more independent outlook. Personal growth can often follow short-term pain. When we help our children learn to respond to problems in a constructive way, we help them acquire a vital life skill.

Competition becomes more significant to our children in their mid to late teens when they have the skills and composure to play under pressure. By then they have the maturity to understand the game. This is about the same time that some of us set aside the role of mom or dad to become an "agent" for our child—especially when the college application process approaches. When we dedicate ourselves to finding the "best team," one that will provide the most exposure for our child, we need to remember that the child is the one who will—or will not—be playing. Many students use college as a stepping-off point to grow in new directions. Whether these years are a time for quiet encouragement or for some desired collaboration toward further skill development, we can—and must—take our cues from our children.

We live in a "quick fix society" as evident in youth sports where trophies proliferate, emphasizing the importance of winning. Some parents–and kids–want to win the wrong things. They prize the $5.00 trophy over the development of their children through a sport. All learning takes time, effort and practice. The real prizes are enjoyment of the subject and the satisfaction of personal growth, something we each must achieve for ourselves.

See also: Anger, Push for Success, School Rivalry, Stress

Stress: Living with The Inevitable

"Our family lives on stress," a mother on the soccer field recently joked. "I'm a doctor, my husband is a lawyer, all our kids are high achievers in school and busy with sports. Heck, even our cat is stressed out!"

It's hard to find a family in Washington that isn't stressed out at least some of the time. Statistically, Washingtonians log one of the longest average work-weeks in the country, and the percentage of working mothers is one of the highest anywhere. Principals often sigh wistfully when they reminisce about the "good old days" when stay-at-home moms were available to volunteer in schools instead of fighting traffic on the beltway just to make it to school in time to pick up their children from after-care.

But while stress is a normal part of life, experts caution that it can be dangerous and even deadly when it gets out of hand, leading to depression and sometimes even suicide. Parents must be particularly observant when the problems and hassles of everyday life start to feel overwhelming to children, transforming some things that may seem fairly trivial into sources of extreme anxiety. The children who are most successful in coping with stress, experts say, are those with supportive and understanding parents.

Symptoms of stress vary, of course, depending on the development level of the child. Elementary school children look at life far differently than teenagers, who are trying to establish their social and sexual identity. Younger school children are dealing with the pressures at home as well as learning to cope with a larger world that involves school and friends. They may feel stressed by things like being teased about an unusual name or nickname, being too short or too tall, not doing well on a test or having a fight with a friend. But parents should not simply dismiss these kinds of stresses as trivial. To the child, they are very real and important. Understanding the issues and validating the child's feelings will go a long way toward building trust and helping your child learn how to cope with life's challenges.

Help kids cope

Building a firm base of understanding and mutual respect will come in particularly handy when your child becomes a teenager. The increased pressure from friends, teachers, coaches and, yes, even parents, can combine to make teenagers feel overwhelmed and stressed out. Parents must realize that teenagers need to take greater control over their own lives, including their scheduling, if they are to learn to cope with life. "What we fail to realize is that parents are sometimes the source of a lot of stress for teenagers," said one parent. "From our expectations for their futures to the fact that we scheduled a dental appointment at a time that conflicts with basketball practice, we add a lot of stress to our teenagers' lives."

Dr. Pamela Campbell, Medical Director of the Children's Hospital Psychiatric Day Treatment Center in Montgomery County, says that the first step in helping children cope with stress is to learn to accept the temperament and personality of each child. All too familiar, she says, is the shy child whose parents are trying to force him to be social, the unathletic child whose parents force him to play Little League or the academically average child with high-achieving parents. "Forcing a child to engage in activities for which she is temperamentally unsuited can lead to anxiety and depression," she says.

Strategies for coping with stress:

- *Teach your child to verbalize his frustration.* If your child responds to stress in a negative way, such as throwing a tantrum or acting out aggressively, give him a pillow to punch instead of another kid.

- *Don't deny that problems exist.* If something is wrong, whether it's a conflict between spouses, illness or money problems, children sense family tension and frequently assume they are to blame. Figure out what to tell your child; if needed, get help from a professional.

- *Lighten up! Make time for fun,* especially with the family. Recreational activities are good stress-busters for kids of any age and their parents.

- *Give your children the opportunity to express themselves,* even if you don't like their choices. Realize that they will make mistakes and that your role is to educate your children so they can make good choices.

While you may not like that nose ring or Mohawk, it's better to develop a sense of humor and patience than to become embroiled in endless conflict over appearance. An open discussion will accomplish more than forbidding, lecturing or grounding.

Especially for teenagers, Dr. Campbell urges a lot of listening and some "space." "Let your child experiment with new ideas, and leave difficult issues open for discussion. If you try to control them too much, they'll rebel just to get revenge," she cautions. But don't be afraid to set limits. "Give them room, but still provide guidelines. You are the parent, not a friend," she adds.

When to intervene

Sometimes, however, stress goes too far. How do you know when to seek professional help? Mental health professionals say parents should seek intervention when a child:

- Seems consistently unhappy and/or cries a lot.
- Eats too much or too little.
- Loses interest in things she used to enjoy.
- Fails or shows a drop in school performance.
- Sleeps too much or too little.
- Withdraws from after-school or social activities.
- Engages in substances abuse, destructive or illegal behavior.

The Washington area abounds with resources to help families deal with stress, depression and related issues. The best places to

start are probably with your child's teachers and school counselor
or get a recommendation from a family physician or trusted friend.

See also: Depression, Friendships,
Push for Success, Sorrow, Sports

Vandalism

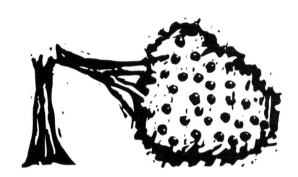

Mother: Johnny, Sam's here to pick you up. You boys be careful and try and be home by midnight.

Johnny and Sam: OK, we will.

Mother: Sam, why on earth do you have so many cans of spray paint on your back seat?

Sam: Oh, uh, I went to the store for my dad. He's going to do some painting in our basement.

Mother: Well, aren't you a great son, helping your dad like that!

Vandalism is an act committed by any person who willfully and maliciously destroys, injures or defaces any real or personal property of another. Graffiti, or "tagging," is the malicious destruction of property. It is a criminal offense.

It's a popular idea that vandalism is just mischief and has no real victim. This idea ignores the anger, fear, frustration and outrage of the people whose property is destroyed. This also doesn't take into account the enormous cost involved in the repair, cleanup and replacement of vandalized property. A rival school's colors or name spray painted before or after a "big game" may incite retaliation resulting in physical injuries and even further destruction of property.

Most vandals are young people, often working in groups, who damage property as a result of boredom, anger, revenge or to show defiance of rules and authority. Some want to draw attention to a cause or their school or group. Local police observe that graffiti is frequently the first sign of gang activity.

Vandalism can have severe consequences. Eggs left on aluminum siding or cars can permanently damage the siding and ruin the paint. A firecracker placed in a mailbox as a prank could seriously injure or kill an unsuspecting passerby. Schools pay out millions of dollars each year to clean up graffiti, repair buildings and replace vandalized equipment. This means less money for new books, computers, athletic equipment and student activities, and could result in higher tuition for independent schools.

Vandalism is a crime!

According to the Youth Services Investigation Division of Montgomery County, a juvenile convicted of vandalism will be required to pay restitution, and may have to serve community service hours, or even appear in juvenile court. The penalties are serious. In Maryland, for damage up to $300, the perpetrator is subject to a fine of up to $500 and a jail term of up to 60 days, or both. If the damage is over $300, the fine could be up to $2,500 and the jail term up to 3 years, or both. If convicted, a juvenile's parents can be held responsible along with the convicted juvenile for restitution of damages up to $10,000.

In 1994 the Montgomery County Council enacted a law which prohibits the application of graffiti on any publicly owned or privately owned surface and prohibits the possession of graffiti material, if it can be shown that the person intended to apply graffiti. The perpetrator is subject to a $1,000 fine, a jail term of 6 months, or both.

Preventing vandalism

- Know where your children are, who they are with, and what they are doing.
- Educate your children about the costs and penalties related to vandalism.
- Look for the warning signs of vandalism or graffiti: possession of spray paint, large quantities of eggs or toilet paper, unexplained paint-stained clothing or hands.
- Protect your house or apartment by using good lighting, locking gates and garages.

If your property is vandalized:

- Report vandalism you witness to the police, school authority, or someone who can take action.

- Inventory vandalism on your property, take pictures of the damage, file a police report, and clean it up as soon as possible, keeping a record of expenditures.

Children who vandalize are children calling out for attention and help. Our job is to know our children and to take appropriate action before there is trouble. We have more to save than property.

See also: Anger, Friendships, Harassment, School Rivalry, Risky Business, Stress

Yes! Doing the Right Thing

Bringing up ethical children is not about having "good" children who do their homework and make their beds. It's about training our daughters and sons to do good, to do the right thing, to be decent and honorable. It's about being a mensch–the Yiddish word for a genuine, worthy, humane person.

One of our main jobs as parents is raising children who have the knowledge and confidence to make wise decisions. Although we have given our children choices since they were small–"Which socks would you like to wear today?" "Would you rather have chicken soup or minestrone?"–as they grow, the choices become more complex–"Should I go to the party when my best friend was left out?" The underpinning for successful decision-making comes from the structure we provide.

Much conventional wisdom about teaching positive values and character to our children and teens is prescriptive and mechanistic. Much of it consists of variations on the simplistic theme of "just say no." Adolescent issues, in particular, don't lend themselves to prescriptive statements that we can coach our children to say when faced with difficult choices. Our central concern might better be how we can empower our children to confidently say "yes."

The most powerful tools we have are our own examples. Do we volunteer to carpool for a sick neighbor? How often do our children see us speak up for a person or issue that needs championing? When we're faced with saving a few dollars or being honest–"Just say you're ten years old; the box office clerk will never know," which do we choose? How do we treat our closest relatives? Do our children look forward to spending time with family, or do they find it a chore? For better or for worse, our children provide miniature mirrors of ourselves. What we do is what we get.

Competency is the soil where our examples can take root. As our children's cognitive, emotional and behavioral competence develops, their capacity to make skillful choices increases. They are less likely to join a group that bullies or belittles others if they feel socially comfortable and emotionally valued by us. Just as we help to support their expanding academic skills, we need to be there to nurture their "goodness quotient."

Another tool we can offer is the age-old reversibility test: "How would you feel it if were done to you?" and the follow-up, "How can you improve the situation?" Interior monologues are also helpful: "Does this choice serve the common good? What would?" When our children grow up seeing the world around them as a place influenced by people's choices, they begin to think of situations as having a selection of outcomes. The training we provide empowers them to do the selecting.

Life gives our children ample opportunities to make decisions and to face challenges–many opportunities to choose to do "the right thing." This is one way they learn to trust themselves, to know how affirming it is to do the right thing. Those same opportunities give us solid evidence to know we can trust them.

Character

We want our children to choose the right behavior–the honest, fair, moral, respectful, responsible choice. We want our children to have good character, what Tom Lickona, author and educator, identifies as the "basic human values that transcend religious, political and cultural differences and express our common humanity."

And we need to tell our children the truth–that it's not always easy to act on the right choice. Some opportunities or invitations to cheat/drink/lie/steal are very seductive. Choosing to do the "right thing" can take enormous strength of character. It's often easier to *know* what's right than to act on it.

The character-building we do is never finished in a day or a year. It is the daily brick-by-brick work that we can admire and affect as it grows. When we reinforce our children's positive choices as well as their positive qualities, we gird them for the tougher times ahead. When they have the security of our support, the strength of our examples and the tools to measure their choices, they can skillfully finish the construction we have carefully begun.

RESOURCES

A Call to Character, eds. Colin Greer and Herbert Kohl, New York: Harper-Collins. 1995.

Golden Rules: The Ten Ethical Values Parents Need to Teach Their Children, Wayne Dosick. Harper San Francisco. 1995.

The Moral Compass: Stories for a Life's Journey. William J. Bennett. New York: Simon & Schuster. 1995.

Resources

ABUSED PERSONS PROGRAMS

DC (202) 576-6762; MD (301) 654-1881; VA (703) 246-7400

Child Abuse: DC Children's Hospital (202) 745-4100
MD (301) 217-4417; VA (703) 246-7400

CRISIS CENTERS

DC (202) 223-2255; MD (301) 656-9161, (TTD)(301) 656-1412; VA (703) 527-4077

Rape/Sexual Assault Victim Crisis Lines: DC (202) 333-7273; MD (301) 656-9420

Suicide: DC (202) 561-7000; MD (301) 738-2255; VA (703) 527-4077

Runaways

Andromeda Spanish Hotline: (202) 291-4707

Child Find of America, Inc.: 1-800-I-AM-LOST (426-5678)

National Runaway Switchboard :1-800-621-4000

Open Door Runaway Program: (301) 770-0193

Teen Hotlines

Alternative House: (703) 356-6360

Maryland Teen Hotline: (301) 738-9697

Maryland Youth Crisis Hotline: 1-800-422-0009

Runaway Hotline: (703) 548-8845

Sasha Bruce House: (202) 546-4900

FAMILIES

Family Support Center: (301) 718-2467
Helps school staff and families prevent, recognize, and overcome mental health and
behavior problems in children and adolescents.

Baby-Sitting Classes

Jewish Community Center of Greater Washington (301) 881-0100

MD Suburban Hospital (301) 896-3939; Montgomery General Hospital (301) 598-9815

VA Red Cross Alexandria (703) 549-8300, Arlington (703) 527-3010

HEALTH

Poison Control:

DC (202) 625-3333; *MD* 1-800-492-2414; *VA* (703) 698-3600

Pregnancy

Birthright (301) 946-3339; HOPE (703) 536-2020

Columbia Hospital For Women (202) 293-6500; Planned Parenthood (202) 347-8512

Rockville Community Clinic (301) 340-9666

Sexually Transmitted Diseases

AIDS 1-800-342-AIDS

STD Line (202) VD2-7000 (832-7000)

VD Hotline 1-800-227-8922

Whitman Walker Clinic (202) 332-5295, Info Line (202) 332-AIDS (2437)

- - - - - - - - -

ADDITIONAL RESOURCES

Alcohol & Other Drugs, p. 20

Anger, p.33-34

Computers, p.53-54

Date Rape, p.65

Driving, p.75

Eating Healthy, p.81

Gender: Raising Boys & Girls, p.94

Harassment, p.99

Respect for Diversity, p.127

Risky Business: Seeking Thrills, p.132

Sexual Responsibility, p.141-142

Smoking, p.153

Sorrow: Coping with Loss, p.157-158

Yes! Doing the Right Thing, p.172

The Parents Council of Washington Member Schools

Academy of the Holy Cross

Aidan Montessori School

Alexandria Country Day School

The Barrie School

The Bullis School

Browne Academy

Burgundy Farm Country Day School

Capitol Hill Day School

Charles E. Smith Jewish Day School

Christ Episcopal School

Commonwealth Academy

Congressional Schools of Virginia

Connelly School of the Holy Child

Edmund Burke School

Episcopal High School

The Field School

Flint Hill School

Foxcroft School

Georgetown Day School

Georgetown Preparatory School

Georgetown Visitation Preparatory School

Gonzaga College High School

Good Counsel High School

Grace Episcopal Day School

Green Acres School

Green Hedges School

Holton-Arms School

Lab School of Washington

Landon School

The Langley School

Little Flower School

Madeira School

Maret School

Mater Dei School

McLean School of Maryland

National Cathedral School

National Presbyterian School

Newport School

Norwood School

The Owl Elementary School

Parkmont School

The Potomac School

Queen Anne School

St. Albans School

St. Andrew's Episcopal School

St. Anselm's Abbey School

St. Patrick's Episcopal Day School

St. Stephen's & St. Agnes School

Sandy Spring Friends School

Sheridan School

Sidwell Friends School

Stone Ridge School of Sacred Heart

Washington Episcopal School

Washington Ethical High School

Washington International School

Washington Waldorf School

The Woods Academy